UNDERSTANDING
THE OLD TESTAMENT

Robert D. Miller II, PhD

Published by
THE GREAT COURSES

www.thegreatcourses.com

Corporate Headquarters:
Phone: 1.800.832.2412
Fax: 703.378.3819
4840 Westfields Boulevard, Suite 500
Chantilly, Virginia, 20151-2299

Copyright © The Teaching Company, 2019
Printed in the United States of America

This book is in copyright. All rights reserved. Without limiting the rights under copyright reserved above, no part of this publication may be reproduced, stored in or introduced into a retrieval system, or transmitted, in any form, or by any means (electronic, mechanical, photocopying, recording, or otherwise), without the prior written permission of The Teaching Company.

Robert D. Miller II, PhD
Ordinary Professor of Old Testament
The Catholic University of America

Robert D. Miller II is Ordinary Professor of Old Testament at The Catholic University of America. He received a PhD in Biblical and Near Eastern Studies from the University of Michigan. He is a research associate at the University of Pretoria and a life member of St John's College Cambridge.

Professor Miller is a scholar of the history, literature, religion, and archaeology of ancient Israel. His books *Chieftains of the Highland Clans: A History of Israel in the 12th and 11th Centuries BC* and *Oral Tradition in Ancient Israel*, as well as related articles, made him a recognized authority on early Israel. Other books by him include *Covenant and Grace in the Old Testament: Assyrian Propaganda and Israelite Faith* and *The Dragon, the Mountain, and the Nations: An Old Testament Myth, Its Origins, and Its Afterlives*.

Professor Miller has worked in the interface of science and theology as the recipient of two major grants in that area, and he participates in Jewish-Christian and Muslim-Christian dialogue at local and international levels. He is a former member of the board of trustees of the American Schools of Oriental Research and was one of the translators of the New American Bible Revised Edition. In 2015, he received the Teacher of the Year Award from his university's School of Theology and Religious Studies Student Association. ■

TABLE OF CONTENTS

INTRODUCTION
Professor Biography | i

Course Scope | 1

LECTURE GUIDES

Lecture 1
The Old Testament as Literature | 3

Lecture 2
The Genesis Creation Story | 7

Lecture 3
What God Intended for Adam and Eve | 14

Lecture 4
When Things Go Wrong in the Garden of Eden | 19

Lecture 5
Abraham, the Father of Three Faiths | 25

Lecture 6
Moses and the Exodus | 31

Quiz 1 | 36

Lecture 7
The Ten Commandments | 38

Lecture 8
The Covenant Code in Exodus | 43

Lecture 9
Leviticus at a Crossroads | 49

Lecture 10
Deuteronomy to Kings | 55

Lecture 11
The Book of Judges | 62

Lecture 12
The Books of Samuel | 71

Quiz 2 | 78

Lecture 13
The Books of Kings | 80

Lecture 14
Biblical Short Stories: Ruth and Esther | 89

Lecture 15
Amos, Prophet of Justice | 96

Lecture 16
The Prophet Isaiah in Three Movements | 101

Lecture 17
Jeremiah, Persecuted Prophet | 105

Lecture 18
Daniel and Apocalyptic Literature | 110

Quiz 3 | 116

Lecture 19
How Scholars Study Psalms | 118

Lecture 20
The Music of the Psalms | 124

Lecture 21
Proverbs in the Bible: Wisdom Literature | 128

Lecture 22
Job's Suffering and Understanding | 132

Lecture 23
Ecclesiastes and the "Vanity of Vanities" | 138

Lecture 24
Slaying the Dragons of the Old Testament | 142

Quiz 4 | 148

SUPPLEMENTARY MATERIALS
Bibliography | 150

Image Credits | 160

UNDERSTANDING THE OLD TESTAMENT

COURSE SCOPE

Christians and Jews share a set of sacred writings that Christians call the Old Testament and Jews call the Tanakh or Hebrew Bible. Written in Hebrew by ancient Israelites over the course of many centuries, the Old Testament is a collection of literature of multiple genres: narrative, philosophy, poetry, invective, history, and mystic vision. The books of this collection reveal a historic people and have served as a basis for art, literature, law, and belief in Western society to this day.

This course provides an understanding of these writings. On one hand, this understanding is based on reading within the context of the ancient Near East. That context includes the historical context as revealed by the discoveries of archaeology and the intellectual context revealed by the writings of ancient Egypt, Canaan, and Mesopotamia.

The history of Israel will emerge from this reading. The similarities and contrasts between the Old Testament—Israel's literature—and the literature and worldviews of Israel's neighbors provide interpretive keys to the text.

UNDERSTANDING THE OLD TESTAMENT

On the other hand, the course also considers the Old Testament as a work of great literature that has the capacity to transcend time and place. Although the origin and development of the biblical books are discussed, the course's primary focus is on the final form of the text, providing a coherent reading of the text that has been handed down to us.

The history of that transmission—the centuries of Jewish, Christian, Islamic, and secular commentary on and creative retellings of the Old Testament—will be charted. That interpretive heritage is presented both for what light it sheds on the text itself and to enable us to see how those re-readings have shaped the intellectual and artistic heritage we have today.

The structure of the course is designed according to three stratagems. The first is the exploration of biblical books that provide the basic story of ancient Israel: Genesis, Exodus, Judges, Samuel, and Kings. This will lead us from Abraham's migration to Canaan, Moses leading the Israelites out of Egypt, the conquest of Canaan, and the history of Israel and Judah through to the Babylonian exile.

Next comes a sampling of books that show the breadth of genres contained within the Old Testament, including Amos, Ruth, Esther, Proverbs, and Daniel. Prophecy, novella, aphorism, apocalyptic vision, and questioning the meaning of life are all here.

Finally, the course examines books whose contents have been foundational for Judaism, Christianity, and the Western intellectual tradition, including Leviticus, Psalms, and Job. These are books that lay behind Judaism's dietary laws, centuries of classical music, and dramatic works of 20th-century playwrights. ■

THE OLD TESTAMENT AS LITERATURE

LECTURE 1

"In the beginning." That's how the Bible starts off, and it seems natural. However, the religious literature of many ancient peoples does not begin with the story of creation. There is a story of creation in the Qur'an, the sacred book of Islam. It's not in the opening chapters. There is a creation story in Hinduism's most holy scriptures, the Rigveda. It, too, is not at the beginning.

There is a point to putting the creation story first. Putting the story of creation first is a way of stating the philosophical truth that Israel's God is not limited to Israel alone. Israel's God is the creator of everything.

UNDERSTANDING THE OLD TESTAMENT

Viewing the Text

It is sometimes best to imagine how one of Israel's ancient neighbors would have seen this text. An immediate question, upon hearing of God creating, might have been: Where did this God come from?

The book of Genesis begins, from a comparative literature perspective, in mid-story. All ancient creation accounts of the ancient Near East told the reader how the gods came to be. That's called a theogony, and Genesis doesn't have one. There is no story of the origin of the Israelite God, named Yahweh.

That absence of a theogony is a theological point. This is the first of many ways Israel broke with the mythology of their neighbors. One of the points of this text is that the world is not made up of mutually opposed forces, the sun and moon are not deities, and the sky is not full of divinities. The entire world comes from one God.

LECTURE 1 | THE OLD TESTAMENT AS LITERATURE

Creating the World

The book of Genesis shows a pattern over six days. (There are seven days of creation, but the seventh is covered in a separate lecture.) Each of the first six days has God participating in a creative act and delivering a verdict (or not). The first three days give form to the formless; the second three days fill the void.

This section features repetition. However, the second three days are different from the first three days. God delivers verdicts on the creations of each day, and the second three are better than the first three.

The structure focuses the reader's attention on verse 26—that is, on human creation. Everything is leading up to the creation of mankind. And only when humanity is in the world does everything become very good.

Days	1	2	3	4	5	6
What is created?	Light	Expanse	Land/plants	Lamps	Sea of creatures	Land animals/humanity
Where?		Water	Land	Sky	Water	Land
Separating? (Yes/No)	Yes	Yes	Yes	No	No	No
Verdict? (Good/Bad)	Good		Good/good	Good	Good	Good/very good
Something named?	Day/night	Yes	Yes	No	No	No
Delegated?	No/yes	No/yes	Earth	No	Yes	No/yes
Copies?	No	No		No	Yes	Yes

The Point of the Pattern

The author has gone to great lengths to construct this elaborate pattern. Creation myths are not about how the world came to be; rather, they are about the nature of the universe. For the ancient Israelite author, the nature of the universe is patterned. The universe is orderly.

UNDERSTANDING THE OLD TESTAMENT

The Creation of Adam by Michelangelo, 1512.

The pattern is the point. This elaborate structure says that the universe is an elaborate structure. Another message of this poetic structure is that within the structure of the physical universe, everything leads up to humanity.

Questions to Consider

✿ Is Genesis 1's concept of an orderly universe dependent on an understanding of the physical shape of the cosmos? Is it undermined by that understanding?

✿ Would ancient Israelites hearing Genesis 1 aurally have grasped the pattern and structure at all? If not, is it valid for us to see it here?

Suggested Reading

Perry, *Exploring the Genesis Creation and Fall Stories.*

Smith, *The Priestly Vision of Genesis 1.*

THE GENESIS CREATION STORY

LECTURE 2

This lecture looks at human creation according to chapter 1 of Genesis. It also looks at the portion of the Genesis 1 creation story that runs into the first verses of chapter 2—the unique seventh day of these days of creation, the Sabbath. The lecture also discusses the authorship of Genesis and the other books of the Torah or Pentateuch, the first five books of the Bible.

Genesis 1

Genesis 1 is a creation myth. The purpose of this creation myth is not so much to tell Israelites how the world came to be as it is to tell them what the world is. It's not about what happened at the dawn of time; it's about the nature of the world as it is now.

Genesis 1:26 reads: "God said, 'Let us make man in our image, after our likeness.'" A wealth of ink has been spilled trying to understand that line. The same idea is repeated in verse 27.

Some people think to be made in the image and likeness of God is a substantial statement. It's about something the human has or possesses. Others believe it is a functional statement. It's about something that humans do.

The Substantial View

Under the substantial line of thinking, perhaps people are in the image and likeness of God in that a human possesses reason. God has a rational mind; a human being has a rational mind.

Another facet could be immortality: God is immortal. A human is immortal only going forward, but given Jewish and Christian belief in eternal life, this is one way that the human is like God. A third sense could be a spiritual nature: In addition to being an animal, a human being is more than an animal, like God, in being spirit as well as body.

The Functional View

It is also important to consider functional interpretations of image and likeness. One of these seems to be required by the context of the verses. Here is verse 26 in its entirety: "God said, 'Let us make man in our image, after our likeness. He shall rule the fish of the sea, the birds of the sky, cattle, the whole earth, and the creeping things that creep on earth."

In context, it seems the man is made in the image and likeness of God in that he will rule over the rest of creation. This is a functional interpretation.

More content appears in verse 27. Here we have a snippet of Hebrew poetry: "And God created man in his image, in the image of God he created him; male and female he created them." To say the image of God equals male and female is not a straightforward philosophical statement. One reading of this line is that a roomful of men does not give you an image of God. A roomful of women does not give you an image of God. If you want to know the image of God, you will need men and women both.

LECTURE 2 | THE GENESIS CREATION STORY

Unpacking the Words

Another way to look at the text is to unpack actual Hebrew words. The word that's translated as "image" is *tselem*. The word translated as "likeness" is *demut*.

Demut is the easier word because it means "shadow," and a person's shadow is like the person. The term *demut* indicates that a human is a shadow of God. A human has traits like God, but not nearly to the extent as God.

The other word, *tselem*, is trickier. That word means "idol," which Israelites were not allowed to make. However, the idol here is not thought of as a picture of a god or as being the god themselves, but as the locus where a worshiper could encounter and truly worship that god. When Genesis 1 says that humanity is the *tselem* of God, it's saying if you want to relate to God, relate to your fellow man.

The Seventh Day

The creation story of Genesis 1 runs through the middle of chapter 2, verse 4:

> Heaven and the earth were finished, and all their array. On the seventh day, God finished the work that he had been doing, and he ceased on the seventh day from all the work he had on. And God blessed the seventh day and declared it holy, because on it on ceased [or rested] from all the work of creation that he had done.

The only thing God created on the seventh is the day itself. This is a creation not in space, but in time. For six days, God created in three dimensions, and on the seventh, God created in the fourth. He also made the seventh day holy.

Judaism came to think of the Sabbath as a location in time. On Friday evening, as the Sabbath begins, a worshiper prepares to enter the Sabbath. Twenty-four hours later, the worshiper leaves it.

Genesis was written at a time when Israel had already been practicing the Sabbath. The first Israelites to ever read this passage had been keeping the Sabbath all their lives. This wasn't written to introduce a new holiday.

Imagine that you've been practicing the Sabbath all your life, and for the first time, you encounter these verses. You realize that when you have kept the Sabbath, you have been emulating God. You have been imaging God.

Authorship

Genesis 1 was written certainly at a time when Israel had long been keeping the Sabbath and the other commandments. Additionally, Genesis goes through the creation story all over again: At the beginning of chapter 2, verse 5, there are no animals or humans. They are created again and in a completely different order. This time, humans come first and animals come second.

These facts raise two questions: When was Genesis 1 written, and why are there two creation stories? The answers depend on an understanding of the authorship of Genesis.

LECTURE 2 | THE GENESIS CREATION STORY

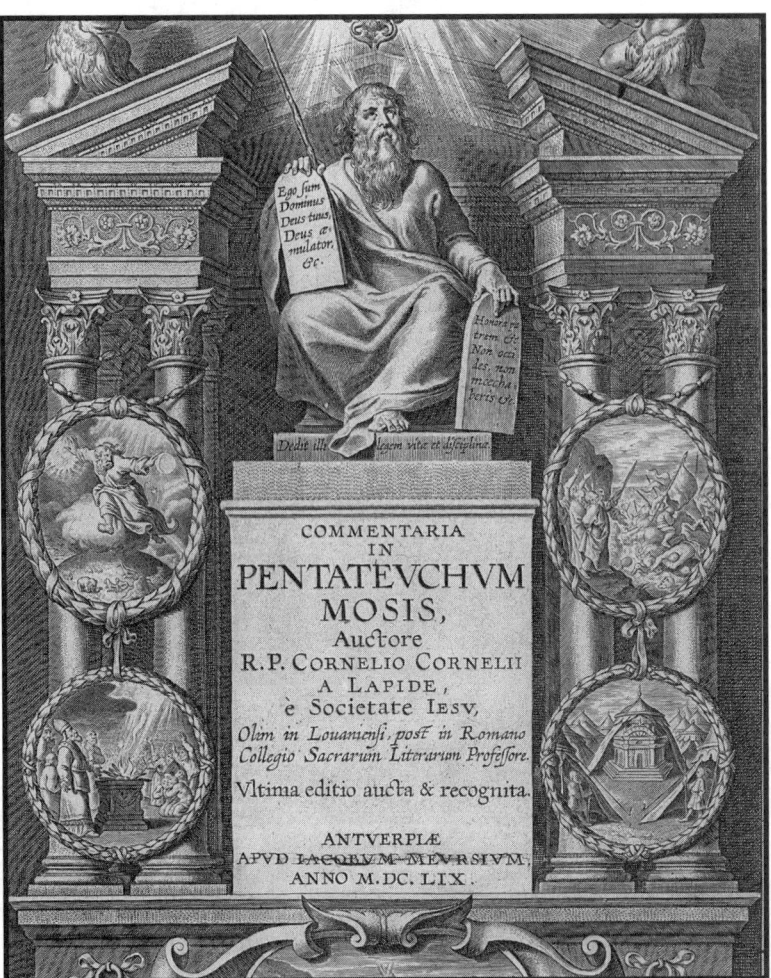

Specifically, it is a question of the authorship of the Pentateuch, the first five books of the Bible that Judaism calls the Torah. It is also sometimes called the five books of Moses. Many Jews, Christians, and Muslims today would espouse the idea that Moses wrote the Pentateuch.

In the 4th century, however, the Christian writer Jerome reported that there were people around him who thought Ezra was responsible at least for the final form of the Pentateuch. Ezra was a priest and scribe who lived in the Persian period around 400 BCE in Jerusalem.

Source Criticism

The modern quest to understand the authorship of the Pentateuch took off in the 18th century, a task called source criticism. The results of that quest are traditionally associated with a 19th-century German scholar named Julius Wellhausen. He did not create this theory, but he brought together work many other people had been doing.

Julius Wellhausen

Exodus 24 serves as a good example, because in it, Moses ends up going up a mountain several times without coming down in between, lending credence to the idea that the text was cut and pasted together from several sources. By first splitting the work into several sources and then uniting them, Wellhausen and those around him eventually came to say there were four sources.

Supposedly, Genesis 1 is the latest of all of the sources, and it comes from around 400 BCE, or the time of Ezra. Chapter 2 of Genesis, on the other hand, is supposedly from the oldest of the four sources, the Yahwist. This was from the 10th century BCE, the time of Solomon. The other two sources fit in between. However, almost no scholar buys this theory anymore.

Nineteenth-century scholars did not strictly address what they considered sources. For Wellhausen, they were authors, making things up from their imagination or information they had heard. An alternative would be to think of them as strictly compilers.

There are other options, however, and now scholars have studied empirically how ancient editing works. They have suggested that ancient editors were neither writers of fiction nor rote copyists, but historians engaged in research, compositionally interweaving oral and written sources, adding marginal notes and expanding. In the end, they were responsible for the wording themselves.

That's important because if the final editor is even at that stage responsible for the wording, then from a certain perspective, the text is all too unified to do source criticism. The entire text is the work of the last editor.

On the other hand, scholars in the last 20 years have also pointed out that the text is really too disparate to do source criticism. In other words, it's one thing to notice that Moses can't go up the mountain if he's already at the top. However, combining the sources from one story with those of another story is extremely subjective, based on perceived similarities in the eye of the beholder.

Source criticism is still very useful. Biblical scholars couldn't work without it. However, the composition of the Pentateuch was more complex as it progressed and more coherent in its final form than past scholarship allowed.

Questions to Consider

- Is the divine decree for humanity to have dominion over the natural world the cause of today's ecological disasters?
- Does the description of human creation in Genesis 1 imply equality of the sexes?

Suggested Reading

Middleton, *The Liberating Image*.

Whybray, *Introduction to the Pentateuch*.

WHAT GOD INTENDED FOR ADAM AND EVE
LECTURE 3

The Israelites did not write philosophical treatises about the nature of the universe and of humanity. Instead, they wrote myths that served as a way of articulating the meaning of life at the time they were written. Genesis 2 and 3 do that with a story. These two chapters are meant to be read together as one creation myth. This lecture covers Genesis 2.

The Early Text of Genesis 2

Genesis 2:5 says that there was no man to till the soil, so God created humanity to till the soil. This comes back up again in verse 15: "The Lord God took the man and placed him in the garden of Eden, to till it and tend it." The Garden of Eden is not envisioned as relaxation and sloth. It's a paradise, but man has a job: to till the soil.

LECTURE 3 | WHAT GOD INTENDED FOR ADAM AND EVE

This part of Genesis also reveals a recipe for creating people: form man from the dust of the earth and then breathe life into him. A human being is material, but a human being also has a divine element.

It is God breathing into man that makes the man alive. However, animals are created from the soil without breath of God, and they are also called living beings. This raises a question: Does it take the breath of God to make a living being, or does it not?

It is possible that there are two kinds of life: life that the animals have and super-life that only comes from the breath. The super-life is lost on the eating of the fruit. Ordinary life lingers on for quite some time afterward. (Note that this is merely one interpretation.)

Additionally, this part of Genesis reveals very confusing directions for the location of Eden. Most Israelites reading the directions would realize how bizarre they are. Perhaps the point of the bizarre travelogue was precisely to keep people from trying to find Eden.

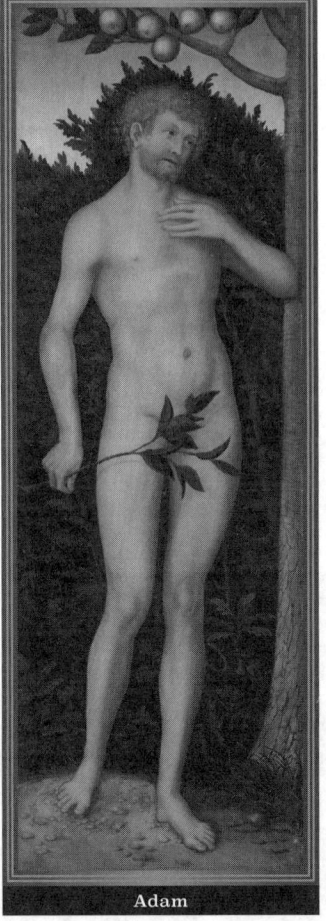

Adam

However, because of what will happen in Genesis 3, readers are supposed to understand these events as taking place in real places. This isn't something that happened in a completely alternate reality. That, in turn, means the decisions that Adam and Eve make are intimately related to decisions real-life people may or may not make.

God gives man the assignment to go and tend the garden in verses 16 and 17. The grammar implies not a permission to eat all trees but one, but a command to eat all trees but one. This is important for the purposes of chapter 3.

UNDERSTANDING THE OLD TESTAMENT

Later Verses of Genesis 2

In verse 18, it is revealed, "The Lord God said, 'It is not good for man to be alone; I will make a fitting helper for him.'" Note that the woman is not a clone of the man. Instead, woman is a being created as both similar and dissimilar to man.

In verse 19, God "formed out of the soil all the wild beasts and all the birds of the sky, and brought them to the man to see what he would call them; and whatever the man called each living creature, that would be its name." Naming was very important in ancient Israel.

Decreeing the name of something was decreeing its purpose and destiny. In Babylonian creation stories, there is a god of wisdom named Enki. In some stories, Enki names plants, people, or regions and thus decrees their purpose in the universe. That divine role here is given to humanity. This is Genesis 2's way of saying humanity has authority over the natural world.

However, the man is not merely possessing. Instead, man is fulfilling that demigod role of decreeing the purpose of each creature in the universe. As the story

EVE

goes on, verse 20 reveals that Adam names the cattle, birds, and "wild beasts; but for Adam no fitting helper was found."

Next, verse 21 says, "So the Lord God cast a deep sleep upon the man; and, while he slept, he took one of his ribs and closed up the flesh at that spot. And the Lord God fashioned the rib that he had taken from the man into a woman; and he brought her to the man."

LECTURE 3 | WHAT GOD INTENDED FOR ADAM AND EVE

Final Verses of Genesis 2

Verse 23 goes on: "Then the man said, 'This one at last is bone of my bones and flesh of my flesh. This one shall be called woman, for from man. She was taken.'" This reveals a pun in Hebrew. The word for man is *Ish* and the word for woman is *Isha*, which also is how you would pronounce "her man."

Verse 24 continues: "Therefore a man leaves his father and mother and clings to his wife, so that they become one flesh." The image here is of monogamy, even though polygamy was legal in ancient Israel. Regardless, the author of Genesis 2 holds that monogamy is the default relationship.

The small problem in this verse is that in ancient Israel, men didn't leave their fathers and mothers. A woman left her father and mother and moved in with a man and his parents. It is possible that the leaving here is psychological rather than residential.

Next, the reader comes to verse 25: "But the two of them were naked, the man and his wife, yet they felt no shame." To a certain extent, this is not meant to sound as ominous as it does, because nakedness in Israelite culture always meant shame. Every time nakedness is used in the Old Testament, it is symbolic of poverty. If the characters are naked, the audience would assume they were ashamed unless told otherwise.

Despite their lack of shame, the lurking threat that there is one tree they shouldn't eat, that they might die, and that perhaps they ought to be ashamed underscores a philosophic argument: The nature of the universe as it has been described in Genesis 2 is meant in the Israelite mind as what ought to be, not what really is.

This is interesting, because in no other ancient Near Eastern creation myth was humanity once living in a different state than now. Every other creation myth explains how the world came to be, and that it is as intended. Genesis 2 is saying the way things are now is not the way God would really have wanted it to be, and it's our fault that it's not.

UNDERSTANDING THE OLD TESTAMENT

Questions to Consider

✡ If the human was created to work in the Garden of Eden, how is this any different from ancient Near Eastern creation myths, where the purpose of humanity is to farm for and feed the gods?

✡ Is woman being made from man in itself suggesting a subordinate creature, regardless of whether he names her or not?

Suggested Reading

Blenkinsopp, *Un-creation, and Re-creation.*

LaCoque, *The Trial of Innocence.*

WHEN THINGS GO WRONG IN THE GARDEN OF EDEN
LECTURE 4

This lecture is about Genesis 3, the second part of the story of Adam and Eve in the Garden of Eden that begins in Genesis 2. Genesis 2 and 3 are a continuous story, which now moves into a second phase, where things go wrong.

The Serpent

Genesis 3:1 describes the serpent as "the shrewdest of all the wild beasts of the Lord God had made." Christianity and Judaism have traditionally read the serpent here as the devil. However, Genesis 3 does not mention the devil or use the name Satan. The serpent isn't the villain of this story; humanity is.

UNDERSTANDING THE OLD TESTAMENT

It's likely that the serpent stands for sorcery—that is, illicit knowledge or infernal wisdom. The Hebrew word for serpent, *nahash*, comes from the same root that means "divination." Divination is not so much magic as trying to gain knowledge by magical means.

On top of that, the serpent in this story is not a snake. It doesn't go on its belly until the end of the story. A snake that doesn't go on its belly is a dragon. When compared to the descriptions of what is called a Nahash in Isaiah 27:1 or Amos 9:3, the serpent is clearly a dragon. That's important, because Israel consistently uses the dragon to symbolize evil. Evil is never a red guy with horns and a pitchfork.

An Israelite reading Genesis 3 would see Nahash and think about chaos or evil. The Israelite would also see "one of the beasts the Lord God had made" and know this creature is meant to be obedient to humanity, not the other way around.

In Genesis 3, the woman tells the serpent, "We may eat of the fruit of the other trees of the garden. It is only about the fruit of the tree in the middle of the garden God said: 'You shall not eat of it or touch it, lest you die.'"

LECTURE 4 | WHEN THINGS GO WRONG IN THE GARDEN OF EDEN

However, that's not what God said. God didn't say anything about touching the tree. Either the man added to the commandment when he told the woman of it, or she has added to it. Either way, the reader is meant to see a problem already.

The Midrash, which is Jewish traditional embellishment of the biblical stories, suggested that by misquoting God, she opened the door to the serpent, who pushed her against the tree. She didn't die, calling into question everything God said. In any case, her embellishment of the law makes it more unreasonable.

The Persuasion Continues

In verse 4, the story continues: "The serpent said to the woman, 'You are not going to die. God knows that as soon as you eat of it, your eyes will be opened and you will be like God [or like gods], knowing good and evil.'"

Everything the serpent has said is technically true, but it is also a lie. Their eyes are opened. They think that sounds like something great, but it isn't. They do know good and evil, but this is also not as good as it sounded. God will say they have become like gods, but it doesn't mean what they thought it meant.

The most important statement of the serpent is "God knows." If God knows you won't die but will gain these wonderful things, then the implication is God does not have your best interests in mind. The serpent portrays God as humanity's enemy without making any explicit accusations.

In verse 6, the woman eats the tree's fruit. She gives three reasons for eating the fruit: She thinks it's good for eating, it's a delight to the eyes, and it will make you wise. Only the third of those came from the serpent. The other two she came up with all by herself.

Verse 7 reads, "And the eyes of both of them were opened, and they knew that they were naked; and they sewed together fig leaves to make themselves loincloths." This is meant to be dark humor: Their eyes were opened to perceive that they were naked.

By verse 11, God has entered the picture and is accusing them: "God said, 'Who told you that you were naked? Have you eaten from the tree which I forbade you to eat from?' The man replied, 'It was the woman you gave to be with me who gave me fruit from the tree, and I ate it.'"

UNDERSTANDING THE OLD TESTAMENT

In one sense, the man is immediately placing blame on the woman. In another sense, he's actually blaming God by pointing out God gave him the woman. The woman tries to pass the blame further on to the serpent.

God Holds Adam and Eve Responsible, Adriaen van der Werff, 1717

LECTURE 4 | WHEN THINGS GO WRONG IN THE GARDEN OF EDEN

God's Verdict

A particular literary structure is present in verses 9 through 19, which is a conversation with God. The verses addressed to the serpent are at the center of this structure. That means these are the most important verses.

This is when the serpent really becomes a snake: "[God said], 'On your belly you will crawl and dust you will eat all the days of your life. I shall put enmity between you and the woman, between your seed and hers. He will strike at your head and you will strike at his heel.'" The idea is this is the beginning of a long conflict between what the serpent symbolizes and humanity.

God's speech continues, with the passage: "'I shall harshen your toil in childbearing; in toil you will bear children. Your passion will be toward your husband, but he will be your master.'" In the next verses, it is revealed that the man will now produce fruit of the fields. There's a parallel between the man's punishment and the woman's: both of them are afflicted with toil.

This is an introduction of patriarchy. Israel was a culture where patriarchy was in question; this text suggests that it is not God's default. It was a sorry result of a break of communion.

Additionally, death comes into play, as God says, "Dust you are … to dust you will return." That obviously envisions death as man's uncreation, because it is reversing the process by which the human was created in Genesis 2. People have reversed God's intention. God is, in some sense, the ultimate victim here.

The Final Verses

Then comes a statement that sounds pleasant but is actually not: "The man named his wife Eve because she was the mother of the living." This naming is another way of saying he owns her and another way of saying patriarchy is now in place.

The final verses of this chapter can be a bit confusing. Take, for example, this passage:

God said, "The man has become like one of us, knowing good and evil; what if he now reaches out and takes fruit from the Tree of Life also, and eats of it and lives forever?" So the Lord God banished him from the Garden of Eden to till the ground from which he had been taken.

It is unlikely that the Israelites understood God here in a petty, jealous way. The words were not supposed to leave readers thinking that the man should have run from the Tree of Knowledge to the Tree of Life before God remembered it was there.

Eating of the Tree of Knowledge has ended the special sort of life that was only supplied by breath from God, absent in the creation of the animals. Eating from the Tree of Life would perpetuate the other sort of living, physical life.

God is worried that the man will live forever in the condition of toil and patriarchy, which would be a fate worse than death. Just as the naming of Eve and covering with skin are not the blessings they look like, the exclusion from the Tree of Life might not be the punishment looks like.

Nevertheless, this is a bad ending. Verse 24 says, "He drove him out and settled him to the east of the Garden of Eden." The word used there for "drove out" is *garesh,* which can also mean "divorce." To be exiled from Eden is a divorce from God, a loss of fellowship with God.

Questions to Consider

- Was the serpent right because everything he predicted came true?
- Cognitive science tells us naked people are more inclined to think about death and to remember they are animals, and that people reminded they are animals are more inclined to think about death. Does this help explain Adam and Eve's knowledge that they were naked?

Suggested Reading

Meyers, *Discovering Eve.*

ABRAHAM, THE FATHER OF THREE FAITHS

LECTURE 5

Abraham—whom God calls to become the father of a new nation in the land of Canaan—is considered the spiritual father of three faiths: Judaism, Christianity, and Islam. For all three, his story illustrates what religious faith means, though there are some differences in how. Those differences underline some of the distinctions of the three modern faiths.

Abraham's Beginning

The story of Abraham truly begins in chapter 12 of Genesis. At this point in the Old Testament, his name is given as Abram. Genesis 12:1 states that God said to Abraham, "'Go from your country and your kindred and your father's house to the land that I will show you. And I will make of you a great nation, and I will bless you and make your name great.'"

UNDERSTANDING THE OLD TESTAMENT

At this point, Abraham is already 75. There is no suggestion in the text that Abraham has met God or knows anything about him. Later Jewish tradition filled in all sorts of stories from Abraham's earlier life, but those are not in the text here.

According to verse 1, Abraham is being asked to relinquish "his land and his family." He is being asked to leave Mesopotamia—that is, ancient Iraq. Essentially, Abraham is asked to relinquish rich mercantile cities for a life of nomadism, leaving behind gold and jade.

Abraham's Journey from Ur to Canaan, József Molnár

LECTURE 5 | ABRAHAM, THE FATHER OF THREE FAITHS

There is no indication that Abraham has any established credentials for this deity that has made this command. He is also an old man, which makes him an atypical pioneer. However, Abraham has faith going for him. He doesn't ask any questions. He simply goes as instructed. This is the first of many examples of Abraham's paradigmatic faith.

Chapter 15

In chapter 15, God reiterates an earlier promise that Abraham will have abundant descendants. God provides him a visual image of how many descendants he will have, but that supplies no basis at all to shore up any confidence. Still, Abraham accepted God as reliable.

Later, God asks Abraham to bring several animals, which are then cut in half and arranged. Then, Abraham falls into a deep sleep. Next, "a smoking fire pot and a flaming torch passed between these pieces. On that day the Lord made a covenant with Abram, saying, 'To your offspring I give this land, from the river of Egypt to the great river, the river Euphrates.'"

The key to understanding this episode is ancient Near Eastern treaties. When two kings were going to make a treaty between their nations, they would take sacrificial animals, then cut the animals in half. Then, the two kings would walk between parts of the animals, reciting the clauses of the treaty.

The ball of fire or smoking fire pot represents God. God passes between the parts of the animals while promising to Abraham aspects of the covenant. However, God does not ask Abraham to pass between the halves of the animals. That's because this is a covenant of divine commitment.

God is making promises to Abraham that are unconditional. There's nothing Abraham has to do in order for God to keep his side of the bargain. Symbolically, God binds himself in this treaty ceremony without asking Abraham to do the same.

Chapter 17

Time goes on, and still Abraham and Sarah have no child. In the intervening chapters, they come up with a creative solution: Abraham sleeps with Sarah's slave, who bears him the son Ishmael. However, God had promised Abraham and Sarah would have children themselves.

In chapter 17, it has been 24 years since God's initial promise. This chapter provides the clearest listing of the three promises of the Abrahamic covenant: progeny, land, and an ongoing relationship between God and Abraham's descendants.

Additionally, in chapter 17, God asks of Abraham and his male descendants that they be circumcised. It reads in verse 14 as if failure to do so negates the covenant. Not being circumcised removes that specific individual from the unconditional covenant with the nation.

Chapter 22

There occurs an important story in chapter 22, after Abraham and Sarah have had their promised child, Isaac. Judaism calls this the *Akedah*, or the "binding" of Isaac. It involves a rigorous task that God asks of Abraham: the sacrifice of Isaac.

However, God is not testing Abraham to see if he has faith. In a certain sense, God is testing Abraham to show Abraham how much faith he himself has. In a second sense, the story is testing God to show how faithful he is. In a third sense, the test is to show Israelite readers something about both Abraham and God.

One should not read this story and conclude that God is a heartless tyrant who doesn't understand human love and affection. In verse 2, God first says that Abraham loves Isaac.

Still, there is a problem with God's command. The command stands in conflict with the promise: How can Abraham have descendants through Isaac if Isaac is dead? If Abraham obeys God, Isaac dies. If Isaac dies, God didn't keep his promise of descendants through Isaac. If God can't keep his promise, why should Abraham obey him? It's a logical paradox.

However, Abraham takes action to prepare to sacrifice Isaac. Just before he does so, though, "the angel of the Lord called to him from heaven and said, 'Abraham, Abraham!' And he said, 'Here I am.' He said, 'Do not lay your hand on the boy or do anything to him, for now I know that you fear God, seeing you have not withheld your son, your only son, from me.'"

LECTURE 5 | ABRAHAM, THE FATHER OF THREE FAITHS

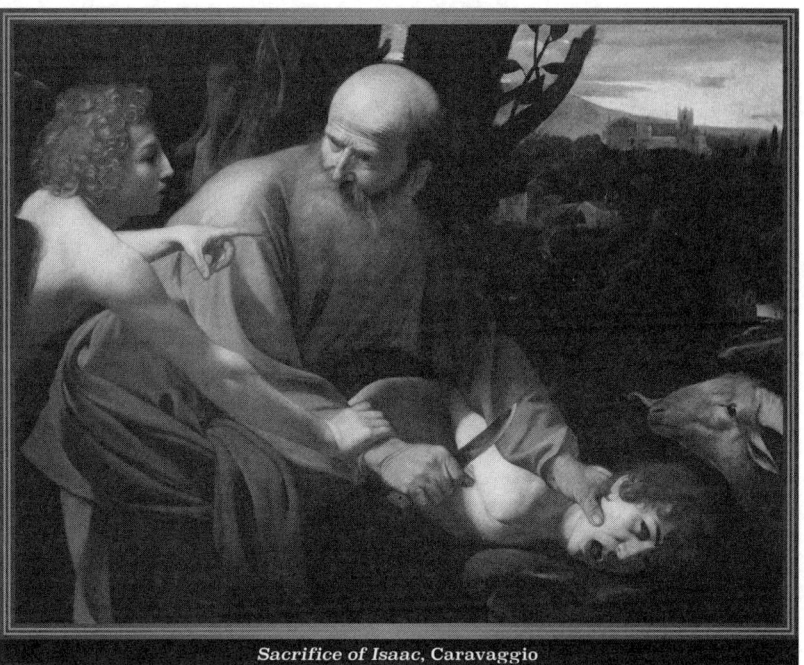

Sacrifice of Isaac, Caravaggio

The Meaning of the Story

In Islam, the story is almost identical. The only difference is that it is the other son, Ishmael, and the events take place not in Jerusalem but at Mecca. Commemoration of this story is the central element of the Haj, the pilgrimage to Mecca required of every Muslim once in their lifetime.

Christian tradition very quickly read this story through the lens of Jesus's death. The first Christians, as Jews, knew this story very well. Christians naturally read this as foreshadowing God willingly offering his son Jesus, who, like Isaac, ends up alive at the end of the story. In one sense, this is allegory, but in another sense, they merely applied what they had always learned reading the story as Jews to a new situation.

For Israelites, the story reinforced the kind of faith Abraham had. It was also a reminder that God provides.

Questions to Consider

✡ What are the issues one must grapple with when applying the land promises to Abraham today?

✡ If God knows he'll tell Abraham not to kill Isaac at the last minute, how is he not a brute playing mind games?

Suggested Reading

Freedman, "Divine Commitment and Human Obligation."

Thompson, *The Historicity of the Patriarchal Narratives*.

MOSES AND THE EXODUS
LECTURE 6

Exodus is the second book of the Old Testament and the second book of the Pentateuch, or Torah. The Exodus is also an event, the act by which Moses—or God—brings the Israelites out of Egypt, which occurs in Exodus in chapters 12, 13, and 14. This lecture addresses key events in the escape.

The Burning Bush

The call of Moses occurs in the episode of the burning bush. This takes place after a baby boy is found floating in a basket. He is given the name Moses and raised in the pharaoh's court. He discovers his Hebrew identity and flees Egypt after killing an Egyptian.

UNDERSTANDING THE OLD TESTAMENT

He is living in the land of Midian, where he's married a Midianite woman, when Chapter 3 begins. It states:

> Now Moses was tending the flock of his father-in-law Jethro, priest of Midian. He led the flock into the wilderness and came to Horeb, the mountain of God. An angel of the Lord appeared to him in a blazing fire out of a bush. He gazed, and there was a bush all aflame, yet the bush was not consumed.

Moses and the Burning Bush, Sébastien Bourdon

LECTURE 6 | MOSES AND THE EXODUS

God's entreaty to Moses is this: "Go back to Egypt and let my people go." Moses's call also serves as a format by which all the prophets are called. His call begins with a blazing bush that does not burn; this is a confrontation with God.

In Moses's case, God interrupts what the prophet is doing. In Jeremiah's case, this occurs in chapter 1, verse 4. In Isaiah's case, it occurs in chapter 6, verses 1–3. With Ezekiel, the encounter starts in chapter 1, verse 1, and it takes the entire chapter.

This similarity is part of what establishes the legitimacy of a prophet. Deuteronomy 18:15—which introduces the concept of a prophet to the Israelite people—states that a prophet is a person like Moses. Moses is the model.

In Exodus 3:4–9, God explains that he has seen his people miserably enslaved in Egypt. That is the grounds for God to call a prophet. There are similar grounds for commissioning in Jeremiah 1:14–19 and in Ezekiel 2:3–5.

Objections and the Sign

In Exodus 3:10, God commands Moses to go to the pharaoh and free the Israelites. In every single prophetic call, the prophet responds with objections, usually having to do with speech. Moses's objections take all of chapter 3, verse 11 through chapter 4, verse 13. God then responds to the objections with reassurance by saying, "I will be with you."

The final segment of the prophetic call is a sign. Moses receives multiple signs so that he can reassure himself and others. With most prophets, the sign has something to do with the lips. The prophet is a messenger for God.

Buried in Moses's call is something else very interesting: the name of God. Moses asks what to tell the followers when they inquire about God's name. God gives the answer in three pieces. Verse 14 begins, "And God said to Moses, 'I am that I am.'"

The rest of verse 14 goes on in this manner: "He continued, 'And you shall say to the Israelites, I am sent me to you.'" Verse 15 looks at the same name from a different angle. God instruct Moses that, "'Thus you shall speak to the Israelites The Lord … has sent me to you.'"

Any English Bible will have the word *Lord* here in small capital letters. The text in Hebrew is the name Yahweh. Most Bibles, by convention, use the word *Lord* in small capital letters because Jews would not write or say the name Yahweh.

The Plagues

Countless arguments have tried to provide naturalistic explanations of the 10 plagues of Exodus. They really go all the way back to 2nd-century BCE Jewish authors such as Artapanus of Alexandria and Philo of Alexandria.

These attempts are wrongheaded for two reasons. The first reason is that if these are natural events, the entire meaning of the passage is lost. These plagues demonstrate the mighty hand of God delivering his people.

The second problem is that these readers are taking the text completely literally. Everything that is described is thought to have happened; it just wasn't miraculous. The idea that everything in the Bible might have happened, but not in a supernatural manner, is strange.

The Israelites Leaving Egypt, David Roberts

LECTURE 6 | MOSES AND THE EXODUS

Some scholars in the last century or so have taken the biblical text stating that God will strike the gods of Egypt—in Exodus 12:12 and Numbers 33:4—to mean that the plagues represent specific attacks on specific Egyptian gods. The Nile turning red is an assault on the god Hapi. The plague of frogs is an assault on the god Heket, and so on. The problem is that in order to make this work, one would have to appeal to rather obscure Egyptian gods—like Heket—that hardly anyone would've worshiped and make connections between gods and plagues that are weak.

However, the theory does work for the last two plagues. The ninth plague is darkness, and the Egyptians worshiped the sun, so the ability to end the sunlight—in other words, directly assault the sun god—is fairly substantial.

Then, the final plague is the death of the firstborn, especially Pharaoh's. Pharaoh was a human version of Osiris, the Egyptian god of resurrection. Still, the other plagues do not match up with the Egyptian gods.

The tendency to want to find naturalistic explanations that support literal historical reading of the text extends to how people read the crossing of the sea. Scholars in the 20th century invented a body of water called the Sea of Reeds. It doesn't exist. If your Bible states in Exodus 15:4 that the Israelites crossed the Sea of Reeds, it has bought into this scholarly construct. The best Bible translations left it as Red Sea.

The Israelites left Egypt as fleeing slaves, and emerged from that sea as a people who could testify forever to God's miraculous deliverance. The result of this deliverance was faith.

Questions to Consider

✡ Why would anyone question a liberation reading of the Exodus, and are they right to do so?

✡ How can God hold Pharaoh responsible for "not letting Israel go" if God "hardens Pharaoh's heart" so that he won't let them go?

Suggested Reading

Huddlestun, "Red Sea."

Saner, *Too Much to Grasp.*

QUIZ 1

1. To sustain the structure of Genesis 1, the authors are forced to have birds created out of:

a. the clouds

b. the sea

c. the fish

d. the earth

2. Genesis 1 says humanity is made as the *tselem* of God, a word ordinarily meaning:

a. an idol

b. a wet clod

c. a puff of smoke

d. salami

3. In Eden, the humans are envisioned as:

a. gardening

b. sleeping

c. playing with the animals

d. reading Torah

4. In "sentencing" Adam for his sin, God curses:

a. Adam

b. Eve

c. the ground

d. himself

QUIZ 1

5. Abraham and Sarah's creative solution to their childlessness is to:

a. have Abraham sleep with Sarah's servant

b. adopt Abraham's servant

c. build a man of clay and put a paper with the name Yahweh on it in its mouth

d. put Abraham to sleep and pull out a rib.

6. Which of the following is not one of the plagues on Egypt?

a. frogs

b. hail

c. darkness

d. mildew

Answers: 1.(b); 2.(a); 3.(a); 4.(c); 5.(a); 6.(d)

THE TEN COMMANDMENTS

LECTURE 7

The Ten Commandments, also known as the Decalogue, have had an elevated status in Judaism and Christianity for a very long time. Those commandments are the subject of this lecture.

The First Commandment

In Exodus chapter 20, verses 1 and 2 state that God brought Israel's people out of Egypt and out of bondage. The first commandment in the text is what God did for Israel, not what Israel is supposed to do for God. The context of the law is God's saving them, which he did before they were keeping any commandments.

LECTURE 7 | THE TEN COMMANDMENTS

In Judaism, verse 2 is counted as the first commandment by itself: "I am the Lord your God who brought you out of the land of Egypt the house of bondage." (The commandments are not given numbers in the text.)

The great Jewish philosopher Maimonides said that this is the first and foremost commandment. It lays down the fundamental of the fundamentals. If a person understands, "I am the Lord your God, who brought you out of the land of Egypt," the person will keep the other commandments.

Verse 3—which is what most Christians see as the first commandment—all the way through verse 6 are considered the second commandment in Judaism. This lecture now turns to the commandments using the Christian numbering.

The First Four Christian Commandments

The first commandment under the Christian numbering is: "You shall have no other gods before me." It has to do with God not wanting to see you have any other deity. This leads right into the next commandment:

> You shall not make for yourself an idol, or a likeness of anything in the heavens above or the earth below. ... You shall not bow down before them or serve them. For I the Lord your God am a jealous God.

When God says, "I am a jealous God," *jealous* is a term arising from the context of human relationships. It's the word one would use to describe a jealous lover, which is an image used to describe God's relationship with Israel throughout the Old Testament.

Verse 7 states, "You shall not invoke the name of the Lord your God in vain." This is a warning that there is no possibility of invoking the name of God without something happening.

The next commandment establishes the Sabbath, starting in verse eight: "Remember the Sabbath day. Keep it holy. Six days you may labor and do all your work, but the seventh day is a Sabbath of the Lord your God." Keep in mind that taking one day off out of seven would have been considered appalling in the ancient world. The Sabbath—as an institution—represents the view that there's something more valuable than human productivity.

Additionally, keep in mind that God rested on the seventh day of creation. This is a reference to Genesis chapter 1. Keeping this commandment teaches us to emulate God.

The Fifth through Ninth Commandments

The fifth commandment instructs people to "Honor your father and mother that you may have a long life in the land the Lord your God is giving you." This is the only commandment that offers a reward, though its meaning is somewhat ambiguous.

The following commandment is deceptively simple: "You shall not kill." In Hebrew, this commandment says you shall not *tirtsah*, which doesn't exactly mean "kill." Some of the very early translations of the Bible had the word *murder* instead, and many translations in the 20th century began to switch to *murder* as well.

The New Revised Standard Version, the Revised English Bible, the New International Version, the New American Standard, and the Jewish Publication Society all state that "You shall not murder."

The verb *tirtsah* is used only 16 times in the Bible. Four of those give no context: It is unclear whether it means "murder" or "kill." Four other times, it means "murder." However, the other eight don't quite fit "murder." It is probably best to leave *tirtsah* translated as "kill" while noting its ambiguity.

The next three commandments are not complicated. They prohibit adultery, theft, and bearing false witness against one's neighbor.

The Tenth Commandment

The tenth commandment provides some complicated restrictions: "You shall not covet your neighbor's wife, his female or male slave, his ox or donkey, or anything that belongs to your neighbor." This is an unenforceable commandment. It legislates a person's thoughts and feelings. This is a reminder that we're looking at a divine lawgiver and not simply at a penal code. The point of this is that a person should regard another's possessions as beyond his possibility of acquisition.

LECTURE 7 | THE TEN COMMANDMENTS

The first commandment is about the hearts and minds, instructing people to have no other gods before God. The last commandment is also about hearts and minds.

The Word *Avad*

A structural element in verse 2 provides the key to the entire text. Consider this: "I am the Lord your God who brought you out of the land of Egypt, out of the land of slavery." The word used to mean *slavery* here is *avad*, which can be translated—and is translated a couple of different ways throughout this chapter.

In every instance of the word *slavery*, *servant*, *slave*, *serve*, or *worship*, the word is *avad*. The term *avad* is used only in a negative sense in the Decalogue: situations where liberty is denied.

The reader is never told to "serve" God. They are told only to not "serve" other gods and images. Each commandment is explicitly—or implicitly—about avoiding putting oneself in servitude to a new pharaoh of any sort. Even God is not a new pharaoh—one is never told to "serve" him.

Keep in mind that the words "commandment" or "law" are never used in the Decalogue. The point of the commandments is to keep Israel from falling into some new house of slavery.

Questions to Consider

✡ How should we translate the commandment: "Thou shalt not kill" or "Thou shalt not murder"?

✡ Does the numbering the commandments are given have any interpretation behind it?

Suggested Reading

Bailey, *"You Shall Not Kill" or "You Shall Not Murder"?*

Heschel, *The Sabbath*.

Meynet, *Called to Freedom*.

THE COVENANT CODE IN EXODUS

LECTURE 8

Among the oldest laws of ancient Israel is the Covenant Code. It is found in the second half of the book of Exodus. This lecture looks at that section of Exodus in an effort to understand the nature of the Torah: the law contained in the first five books of the Bible.

The Scattered Topics of the Covenant Code

Scholars usually say the Covenant Code begins in Exodus 20:22–26, which reads:

> You shall not make alongside of me gods of silver, nor shall you make for yourselves gods of gold. An altar of earth make for me, and

sacrifice upon it your burnt offerings and communion sacrifices. … If you make an altar of stone for me, you shall not ascend to my altar by steps, lest your nakedness be exposed.

These are rules about how to build religious structures. They aren't laws about civil society. Instead, they are something that would be reserved to rubrics of religions.

Matters change in the verses after that. In chapter 21, these instructions are delivered: "When you purchase a Hebrew slave, he is to serve you for six years. In the seventh year, he shall leave as a free person without any payment."

The laws about slavery continue for several verses. Then, the rest of the chapter is primarily about personal injury. It is similar to tort law: We're told what is against the law and how to work out compensatory and punitive damages.

This continues up to chapter 22. That chapter also includes instructions about sorcery, oppression, and dietary law. All in all, the laws seem to have no order to them. They don't have any concept of religion.

There is no Hebrew word meaning "religion" here, and the readers would not have understood a distinction between sacred and secular. They didn't see the world as compartmentalized. Putting these laws together makes the point that all laws are equal; all are divine in origin. There is no distinction in God's eyes, either.

Two Types of Laws

There are two different phrasing styles of laws in the Covenant Code. Scholars divide them between casuistic and apodictic laws. A casuistic law is stated in an if/then format. Apodictic laws have no conditions.

LECTURE 8 | THE COVENANT CODE IN EXODUS

In the early 20th century, scholars thought the apodictic laws were unique to Israel. They're not, because they were also present in ancient Syria. However, casuistic laws were the norm in the ancient Near East, and not simply in terms of style.

Every casuist law found in the Covenant Code has also been found in the cuneiform laws of ancient Babylon—that is, ancient Iraq. In some cases, these parallels are precise.

For example, the beginning of the Code of Hammurabi legislates how to set up worship in temples. Then, it goes into laws about slaves similarly to how the Covenant Code begins.

Laws number 117 and 118 in the Code of Hammurabi are exactly parallel to Exodus 21:2–7. People fell into slavery due to debt. Consequently, "His wife, his son, his daughter, they shall perform service in the house of the buyer or the one who holds them for three years. Release shall be secured in the fourth year."

The Code of Hammurabi talks about what happens to the wife and children just as Exodus does. Many other parallels between the two sources exist as well.

Differences

There are a number of important differences between the Covenant Code and ancient Near Eastern law. First, the Covenant Code broke with Israel's neighbors in having no varying penalties for perpetrators of different classes.

Second, in biblical law, there are no property infringements punishable by death. No type of theft in ancient Israel resulted in the death penalty. On the other hand, there are very few types of homicide where the perpetrator can get away with just a financial penalty.

By contrast, in ancient Near Eastern law, the situation was the exact opposite. In the Middle Assyrian laws that come several centuries later and in the Hittite laws of ancient Turkey, there were many kinds of theft punishable by death. Additionally, there were many forms of homicide in which the perpetrator got away with a financial penalty.

A Close Relationship

There was a close relationship between Israelite law and the ancient Near Eastern laws. This is particularly true of the Code of Hammurabi, although there are parallels with broader ancient Near Eastern laws. Some of the parallels between Covenant Code and the Code of Hammurabi are also found in early Sumerian laws, in Middle Assyrian laws from later than the Code of Hammurabi, and in Hittite laws as well.

Some scholars have argued that there was a common legal tradition for the whole ancient Near East—that is, a shared common law system that lasted thousands of years. That's hard to imagine, however, given changes of culture and language as well as the sheer length of time involved.

On the other extreme, some scholars argue that the Covenant Code was written during the Babylonian exile, when Jews were in captivity after the Babylon king Nebuchadnezzar conquered Jerusalem in 586 BCE. The parallels of the Bible and the Code of Hammurabi are a literary phenomenon based on exiled Jews copying the Code of Hammurabi while they were in Babylon in the 6th century.

There are a number of problems with this theory. Although the Code of Hammurabi was copied many times, there are almost no copies of the Code of Hammurabi during the period of Nebuchadnezzar and his dynasty. The actual laws that were in operation in the Neo-Babylonian world were completely different and don't look at all like Exodus.

Another explanation involves particular laws like Exodus 21:22–25, which covers men fighting and causing a woman to have a miscarriage. This is an unusual situation that appears in Exodus 21, the Code of Hammurabi, the Middle Assyrian laws, Sumerian laws, and Hittite laws.

There is no single legal system covering all these kingdoms, so it is probably better to think of this as a literary phenomenon: as a matter of texts or oral traditions borrowing from other oral traditions.

There are swaths of law missing, and court records of Hammurabi's time include all sorts of conflicts that Hammurabi's code ignores. These court actions never even refer to the code. Instead, they refer to the decision of the king, and often that decision is the opposite of what the code requires.

LECTURE 8 | THE COVENANT CODE IN EXODUS

In other words, it was never a binding law code. It is likely that the scholars who argue that written law did not play a role in the ancient Near East are right. The actual, functioning law was something oral.

No one has been able to prove that Mesopotamian law codes were ever actually used for legal proceedings. More than 40 copies of the Code of Hammurabi have been found, many of them from centuries after Hammurabi. It could hardly have still been used as a legal code. The scholar Raymond Westbrook has argued that the so-called law codes were school texts.

The cases in the Code of Hammurabi and the Covenant Code are so particular because if you're teaching someone law, you want to start with borderline, theoretical scenarios. Then, you can derive ordinary cases easily from the strange ones.

Justice

The Covenant Code in Exodus says slaves still have rights to justice under the law. Most slavery in ancient Israel was private. There was no state slavery or corporate slavery, and most slaves were fellow Israelites, not foreigners. Most people became slaves through debt.

The Code of Hammurabi does not forbid killing one's own slave. Israelite law does. The owner could not unintentionally kill his own slave without the act being avenged, meaning the death penalty. Slaves within the purview of justice and slavery have certain rights.

Chapter 22:20–21, present three other groups in the scope of justice: "You shall not oppress or afflict the resident alien, for you were once aliens residing in the land of Egypt. You shall not wrong the widow or orphan." This triad of widows, orphans, and foreigners is often repeated.

These are three groups of people who have no one looking after them. These three categories are cited together repeatedly in the Old Testament. The text, however, says they're very much within the scope of justice.

The image presented is that they do have a patron: God. He will support the widow, the orphan, and the foreign guest worker. This is more about moral education than a legal code. Specifically, it's about establishing who has a standing within the scope of justice. This curriculum formed the basis of Judaism and reveals some very fundamental notions of human justice.

Questions to Consider

- Does the legality of slavery and treatment of women as property negate any modern relevance of the laws of Exodus?
- What would an ancient Israelite have thought of the similarities of their own law to Babylonian law?

Suggested Reading

Houston, *Contending for Justice*.

Westbrook and Wells, *Law from the Tigris to the Tiber*.

LEVITICUS AT A CROSSROADS
LECTURE 9

Leviticus sits in the middle of the Torah—that is, the first five books of Hebrew scripture. Nearly half of the 613 commandments in the Torah have their basis in the book of Leviticus, so anyone who wants to understand religious Judaism must understand this book.

This lecture looks at three sections of the book, starting with the first part, which deals with the sacrificial system. Then, the lecture turns to a section that scholars call the Manual of Impurities. Finally, the lecture turns to chapter 16 and the Day of Atonement.

The Sacrificial System

The first two chapters of Leviticus describe the sacrificial system that—in theory—was operational in the Jerusalem Temple. Some people ascribe authorship of the book of Leviticus to Moses along with the rest of the Pentateuch, the first five books of the Old Testament.

However, most scholars agree that this book is late, probably put in its final form after the Babylonian exile in the 6th century BCE. Leviticus's sacrifice list is a catalog written after centuries of practice, not directives about how the temple in the Old Testament was to run.

The sacrifice of animals in the temple was rarely thought of as a way to deal with God's need to punish sins. That view is present, but it is far less prominent than making a gift to God of produce of the land or flocks, for example.

The sacrifices fall into five categories. The first in chapter 1 is the burnt offering or whole offering. In Hebrew, it's called *olah*. It's called a whole offering because it's completely burned up and offered to God. Here, scent is far more important than eating. God liked the smell rather than needing to be fed.

LECTURE 9 | LEVITICUS AT A CROSSROADS

The second offering takes place in chapter 2, and it's of grain. In Hebrew, it's called *Minhah*. The grain can be presented in any number of forms. Today, *Minhah* is still the name in Judaism for afternoon prayers.

Chapter 3 brings the next offering: a *shalom* offering. This can be translated as peace offering, but some Bibles translate it as a communion sacrifice. This animal sacrifice can be offered for a number of different reasons, including devotion, vow fulfillment, or thanksgiving to God. A portion of the remains are given to—and eaten—by lay worshipers and the priests. God was seen as an invisible guest at this communal meal.

The sacrifice in chapter 4 is usually called the sin or purification offering. The one in chapter 5 is called the guilt or reparation offering. Both are for unintentional sins. Only the Day of Atonement deals with intentional sins a person later comes to regret.

The Manual of Impurities

Beginning in chapter 10 and running through chapter 15 is the section called the Manual of Impurities. Much of the ancient world had a concept of purity and impurity. This is not the same as good and evil. Uncleanliness is not a malevolent quality as much as it is an aesthetic state. This is why many religions have ritual washing. There is a great deal of ceremonial washing in Judaism and before prayers in Islam.

One of the first sets of regulations we see is the laws of kosher foods—that is, what foods are acceptable and what foods are not. For instance, chapter 11:2 highlights pigs, hyraxes, rabbits, and camels as unclean. Other animals are also restricted.

The American biblical scholar W. F. Albright is correct that no part of the Bible is more clearly based on empirical observation and logic than the book of Leviticus. That comes out in chapter 13 and its extended discussion of leprosy. Leviticus 13:2 references someone with a "lesion, or blotch which appears to develop into a scaly infection."

The subsequent verses contain what is essentially empirical medical inquiry. It includes a large number of technical terms that must have been medical terms at the time, including *mark*, *lesion*, and *blotch*.

Incidentally, the condition is not really leprosy. Doctors who have read through chapter 13 of Leviticus think that it is probably vitiligo or psoriasis instead.

The Day of Atonement

Right in the middle of the book—chapters 16 and 17—is the Day of Atonement, also known as Yom Kippur. There's some debate about how early the Day of Atonement became part of the Israelite calendar. Some of the early calendars of the festivals outside of the book of Leviticus don't list it, but there are some elements that seem very old.

It's complicated to follow what's actually happening in the text. At the beginning of the festival, the high priest—referred to as Aaron, the first high priest and brother of Moses—sacrifices a bull for his sins. Then, he enters into the Holy of Holies, where the Ark of the Covenant was kept, the gold-covered wooden chest containing the tablets of the Law.

The only day in the year when anyone entered the Holy of Holies was the Day of Atonement, when the high priest did so at the beginning of this feast. Next, verse 5 states, "From the Israelite community, he shall receive two male goats for a purification offering." After that, verse 7 says:

> Taking the two male goats and setting them before the Lord at the entrance of the tent of meeting, he shall cast lots to determine which one is for the Lord in which one is for Azazel. The goat determined by lot for the Lord, Aaron shall present an offer up as a purification offering, but the goat determined by lot for Azazel will be placed before the Lord alive so that with it He may make atonement by sending it off into the desert.

There are two goats, and both goats are to atone for the sins of the people, including intentional sins. In verse 15, the high priest slaughters the goat of the people's purification offering and then sprinkles the Ark of the Covenant with its blood.

LECTURE 9 | LEVITICUS AT A CROSSROADS

Jews Praying in the Synagogue on Yom Kippur, by Maurycy Gottlieb (1878)

Verse 16 reveals what is happening: "He shall purge the inner sanctuary of all the Israelites' impurities and trespasses, including all their sin." The role of the sanctuary in the life of the people is in danger of becoming lost, and this goat is offered to remove their sin and impurity to purge the sanctuary.

In verse 20, when the high priest is finished purging the inner sanctuary, the description continues:

> Aaron shall bring forth the live goat, laying both hands on its head. He shall confess over it all the iniquities of the Israelites and their trespasses, including all their sins, and so put them on the goat's head. He will then have it led into the wilderness by an attendant and the goat will carry off all their iniquities to an isolated region.

This section raises some questions: Where are they going, and what does it mean to send the goat off to Azazel in the desert? Scholars do not know for sure. The rabbis argued that Azazel is a place name.

Meanwhile, the late-4th-century Vulgate translation of the Bible from Hebrew into Latin translated Azazel as the noun *escape-goat*, or *scapegoat*. That is where the term came from.

Some of the Apocrypha, or books that didn't make it into the Jewish or Christian canon of the Bible held that Azazel was the name of a demon, or even the chief demon. And there is a suggestion in Leviticus 17:5–7 of demons dwelling in the wilderness. Still, it is impossible to say for sure.

Questions to Consider

- What would have been the theological impact of losing the Jerusalem Temple and its sacrificial system in 586 BCE?
- How would the value of Leviticus for Jews versus for Christians impact dialogue between those two groups today?

Suggested Reading

Zenger, "The Book of Leviticus."

DEUTERONOMY TO KINGS
LECTURE 10

One of the most exciting books of the Old Testament is the book of Judges. It presents a great opportunity to see how the Old Testament relates to the history of ancient Israel, as archaeologists have reconstructed it.

A Standalone Book?

There is some debate over whether Judges is actually a standalone book of the Old Testament. In the mid-1900s, a German scholar named Martin Noth suggested that the Old Testament books of Joshua through the book of 2 Kings should be read as a single unit. That covers Joshua, Judges, 1st and 2nd Samuel, and 1st and 2nd Kings.

Noth coined the phrase Deuteronomistic History for this collection. Likewise, this course treats Joshua through 2 Kings as a unit: the Deuteronomistic History, written by the same people, with the same underlying theology.

Two Accounts

The first two books of the Deuteronomistic History are Joshua and Judges. The books present two different accounts of how Israel came to be in the land of Canaan. The presentations are not contradictory so much as they emphasize different things.

In this way, the Bible gives us different models for understanding how Israel came to be in the land of Canaan, and historians and archaeologists have divided those into four models.

Outside of the Bible, the earliest mention of Israel is found in an Egyptian text called Merneptah Stele, dating from 1220 BCE. A stele is a stone slab erected as a monument, sometimes inscribed. In the Merneptah Stele, the Egyptian pharaoh states: "Israel is laid waste; his seed is no more." That means by 1220, some sort of Israel has to be residing in the land of Canaan. That's where the agreement between scholars ends, leading to the four models.

The Four Models

The Book of Joshua presents a model of a lightning military campaign in the career of a single general, who conquers the cities of Canaan for Israel. This conquest model was endorsed by many scholars in the 1950s, 1960s, and 1970s. Today, few biblical scholars and no archaeologists accept this model.

The reason is this: There are no certain destruction dates of cities of Palestine during the 13th century BCE, except for two, and those are about 100 years apart: the city of Hazor in 1250 and Lachish in 1150. All of the other cities Joshua is said to have conquered either didn't exist at the time, like Jericho or were never destroyed.

Drawing on the book of Judges, mid-20th-century scholars began to propose a second, peaceful migration model. In this view, nomadic Israelites peacefully migrated from the East across the Jordan River into the empty land of the highlands of Canaan and settled down.

LECTURE 10 | DEUTERONOMY TO KINGS

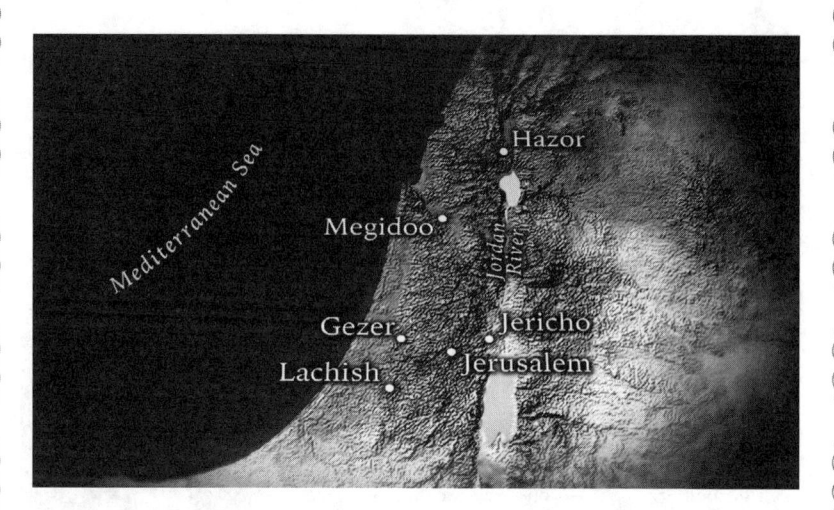

On the one hand, this certainly fits the lack of destroyed cities. On the other hand, nomadic people do not just settle down. More importantly, archaeological evidence does not make the Israelites look like immigrants from anywhere.

In the 1970s, scholars tried to come up with a model that would explain the rise of Israel out of elements of 13th-century Canaanite society. The first of these is usually called the peasant revolt model. The model states that most Israelites were oppressed peasants of the Canaanite lowland cities who revolted and withdrew to the hills under the banner of the God Yahweh who believed everyone was equal. It would be difficult to prove the peasant revolt theory one way or another.

The fourth model takes a bit of all that came before it. It's also the most accurate model. It argues that most Israelites were originally Canaanites or people who had lived alongside the Canaanites for some time. There was, however, an infiltration from the east of several groups into the highlands of Canaan.

These people brought with them the worship of Yahweh, and they mixed with Canaanites. The book of Ruth illustrates, with its stories of intermarriage, this kind of symbiosis, and the fourth model is called the symbiosis model.

Ethnicity

The architecture and pottery of an early Israelite village is largely the same as that in a Canaanite settlement. This raises a question: How do we know one is Israelite and one is Canaanite? That is tied in with the question of how one defines ethnicity in the first place.

Long ago, scholars gave up any notions of ethnicity meaning genealogical affiliation. It's not necessary to share DNA to be part of an ethnic group.

Early non-biological discussions of ethnicity focused on trait lists. In other words, an ethnic group was all the people who shared certain traits, such as styles of dress, pottery, or foodways.

The problem with this is that some clearly ethnic groups do not meet the qualifications, while other sociological groups—such as economic classes or workers societies—would be called ethnic groups. Archaeologists would now agree that ethnicity is self-defined, so it's subjective. However, people define their ethnicity around objective traditions.

Israelite pottery

Israelite and Canaanite pottery are similar, as are other elements, but they're not identical. The highland villages that make up the Israelite contingent have a small subset of all of the pottery and other material goods that Canaanite cities also have. Every piece of pottery or metal found in an Israelite village would be found in a Canaanite city.

However, some of the things one might have found in the Canaanite city would never be found

Canaanite pottery

in one of these highland villages. Even the smallest lowland villages have locally made Egyptian pottery forms as well as large amounts of pottery imported from Cyprus. They have incense stands, cuneiform tablets, and Egyptian hieroglyphic door lintels.

Items like that are never found in any of the highland sites. The difference suggests that the highlands constitute a self-contained ethnicity on stylistic grounds. The Merneptah Stele tells us it was called Israel.

LECTURE 10 | DEUTERONOMY TO KINGS

The Historical Picture

The Early Iron Age covers the years from 1200 to 1000 BCE. During the previous era, the Late Bronze Age, all of Canaan was ruled by Egypt. Beginning around 1200, Egypt became consumed with internal matters. The Egyptians kept control of parts of Canaan until 1150, by which time everything was independent. This allowed several different groups to expand in different parts of the country, generally getting along well with each other.

In the Canaanite communities—including the cities on the coast and Jezreel Valley—town mayors became independent kings. They had control of the coastal highway route up to Jerusalem, which remained a Canaanite city. They did not call the city Jerusalem during this period. They called it Jebus. It was surrounded on the north, east, and south by Israelites.

The entire area from Jerusalem almost to Jenin—the entire northern half of the modern West Bank—was dotted with small villages belonging to the Israelites in the Early Iron Age. That's what the archaeology tells us, and it's also the background for the entire book of Judges.

The Pattern of Judges

The book of Judges is not necessarily arranged chronologically. Its second chapter sets out a pattern by which the book will present, in turn, each of the judges. The pattern starts in Judges 2:11 with Israelites prostrating themselves to other gods, which the text calls "doing what was evil in the Lord's sight."

This invariably was followed by God's anger and the Israelites being handed over to their oppressors, which is seen in verse 13:

> Because they had abandoned the Lord … the anger of the Lord flared up against Israel. He delivered them into the power of plunderers who despoiled them, sold them into the power of the enemies around them. They were no longer able to withstand their enemies. Whenever they marched out, the hand of the Lord turned against them.

The next stages of this pattern are that the people will cry out to God, and he will have compassion and raise up a leader among them. In other words, there's no hereditary leadership. God will select a leader. Those charismatic leaders are the people called judges.

Verse 18 states: "And the Lord raised up judges for them. He would be with the judge and save them from the power of their enemies as long as the judge lived." The judge delivers the people from its enemy. When the judge dies, the process repeats all over again.

As the book of Judges goes on, the amount of time the Israelites are under the control of another power grows progressively longer. The time between when they cry out to God before he actually raises up the judge grows longer. The amount of time between the death of the judge and the arrival of a new oppressor becomes progressively shorter.

Additionally, if the judge is an institution that holds the key to Israel's survival, it's also open to abuse. The judges themselves come to typify the sins of their people. Hints of this appear in the first half of the book. The last part of chapter 3 introduces us to the judge Ehud, who saves Israel from foreign domination—but by assassination.

Ehud

LECTURE 10 | DEUTERONOMY TO KINGS

The next major judge we encounter—in chapters 4 and 5—is Deborah. Her general, Barak seems unnecessarily timid and refuses to go into battle unless Deborah accompanies him. Their disposal of the enemy general depends on assassination, too.

In the second half of the book, things will soon go from bad to worse, as the judges themselves become the ones leading Israel into wickedness. The last third of the book is a slow decline into immorality, violence, and enslavement to other nations. From the perspective of the text, then, Israel doesn't conquer Canaan. Instead, it becomes Canaan.

Questions to Consider

- Does Judges really show the supposed theology of the Deuteronomistic Historian, or are Jephthah and Samson the only people in Judges who follow the Deuteronomy line of thinking?
- Why does the author set out a pattern at the start of the book and then rarely follow it?

Suggested Reading

Campbell and O'Brien, *Unfolding the Deuteronomistic History*.

Shanks, Dever, Halpern, and McCarter, *The Rise of Ancient Israel*.

THE BOOK OF JUDGES
LECTURE 11

The opening of the book of Judges describes a pattern in which the idolatry of Israelites is followed by God leaving them to foreign oppressors. Then, when the people cry out, God raises up a judge, a charismatic leader, who frees them—until they revert to idolatry upon the judge's death. The judges who follow the first judge, Othniel, are leaders who increasingly engage in questionable behaviors themselves. This lecture focuses on the latter parts of the book of Judges.

Gideon

The second half of Judges starts with an extended cycle about the judge Gideon in chapters 6 through 8. Chapter 6 begins according to the pattern the book of Judges sets out at its start. Israel is in the hands of its enemies, and it then cries out to God for help.

LECTURE 11 | THE BOOK OF JUDGES

Gideon is appointed Judge

However, instead of raising a judge, God sends a prophet, whose role is to remind the Israelites that crying out is not itself repentance and that the lord's intervention in their plight is not necessarily assured. However, God does eventually choose Gideon to be the next judge. This sets in motion first a religious reform, and after that, military redemption.

Gideon claims to be unfit to be the next judge because his family is from a weak faction of the Manasseh tribe. The story of Gideon is really about where true power lies. For Gideon, it's about numbers and strength, while God tries to teach him to depend on divine assistance.

Gideon uses one means after another to verify beyond question that God will assist him and provide him with the necessary power to overcome oppressors. Gideon forms an army and leads it off to face the enemy. God spends most of chapter 7 whittling down the army Gideon has just assembled, so that by the time he reaches the enemy, he is left with a very small force. This is to show that any victory will be God's doing, not based on human power.

Once again, Gideon wants reassurance. He sneaks with an assistant into the enemy camp in the second half of chapter 7. Only after hearing a dream related by one of the enemy soldiers does he seem to grasp and accept God's power behind him.

However, God more or less disappears from Gideon's story at this point. Having been reticent and rather cowardly so far, Gideon is now a gung-ho commander. With God in the background, he initiates a series of far-flung, mopping-up operations.

When all of this is finished, the Israelites say to Gideon: "Rule over us, you, your son, and your son sons, for you saved us from the power of Midian," giving no credit to God. Gideon answers that God must rule.

Gideon goes on to ask for a large amount of gold. We are then told: "Gideon made an ephod out of the gold and placed it in his city Ophrah." Here, the ephod is some idolatrous object of worship. The rest of the verse states, "and all Israel prostituted themselves there, and it became a snare to Gideon and his household."

At the start of his career, Gideon turned the people away from idolatry, demolishing their Baal shrine. At its end, he turned them to a new sort of idolatry, leading them to worship the gold ephod he'd made—pretty much the exact opposite of what a judge is supposed to do.

Abimelech

In chapter 9, the story leads to Gideon's son, Abimelech. His name means "my father is king," and that must be important, because the name is repeated 31 times in the text. Abimelech makes himself king.

LECTURE 11 | THE BOOK OF JUDGES

The story of Abimelech is the structural center of the book of Judges. This book opens by stating that there was no king in Israel, and everyone did as they saw fit. In the middle, the book shows a monarchy that is not any better. Abimelech has none of Gideon's good qualities and all of the bad, especially repeating his military overreactions.

The basic story of Abimelech is that the town of Shechem makes Abimelech king, but quickly turns against him. Abimelech and his gang destroy most of the city—which apparently is not an Israelite town—along with its ruling class. However, Abimelech himself is then killed on a campaign to another city further north.

The overall Gideon-Abimelech narrative is a magnifying glass on infidelity, including infidelity to God and infidelity to Gideon, as Abimelech has all of his brothers assassinated. When people turn finally against Abimelech, it leads to an increase in civil strife.

Abimelech's Death

Jephthah

If Abimelech is the most brutal judge, the next one, Jephthah, is the most pitiable. Chapter 10 describes God handing Israel over to its enemy, the Ammonites. In chapter 11, God raises Jephthah as a judge.

He starts off looking better than Abimelech and Gideon. He tries diplomacy in Judges 11:12–28. He negotiates with the Ammonites about a piece of land that was claimed by Israel and Ammon. Israel had taken it long ago from people called Amorites. Jephthah wants to argue that it belongs to Israel, but he has many of the events wrong.

Later, Jephthah makes a vow in chapter 12, verse 30. He says, "If you deliver the Ammonites into my power, whatever comes out the doors of my house to meet me when I return from the Ammonites in peace shall belong to the Lord. I shall offer it up as a burnt offering." Jephthah is successful. In verse 34, this occurs:

> When Jephthah returned to his house in Mizpah, it was his daughter who came out to meet him with tambourine playing and dancing. She was his only child. He had neither son or daughter besides her. When he saw her, he tore his garments and said "Oh my daughter! You have struck me down and brought calamity upon me, for I have made a vow to the Lord and I cannot take it back."
>
> "Father," she replied, "you have made a vow to the Lord. Do with me as you have vowed because the Lord has taken vengeance for you against your enemies the Ammonites."

This episode concludes with: "He did to her as he had vowed." This is a tragic ending. The vow and whether it should have been binding troubled early Christian and Jewish theologians.

Some medieval theologians pointed out that it only says, "He did as he had vowed"—not explicitly that he killed her. Perhaps he didn't actually kill her, but instead put her away in a cloister, much like a nun in a convent. However, most earlier Christian and Jewish writers knew it was an actual killing.

LECTURE 11 | THE BOOK OF JUDGES

Jephthah returning from Battle is greeted by his Daughter,
Giovanni Antonio Pellegrini, 1708 - 1713

The rabbis and the 4th-century Christian writer Augustine said Jephthah should never have made a vow like that in the first place. However, Augustine goes on to praise Jephthah for keeping the vow. Other theologians, Christians and Jewish, considered the vow and its fulfillment both reprehensible.

Samson

Chapter of 13 of Judges opens with Israel again under foreign oppression by the Philistines, who ruled along the Mediterranean coast of Canaan. The Israelites in this story don't show much sign of wanting to be set free from the Philistines. The figure of Samson is more interested in sleeping with the Philistines than fighting them, until God forces him to.

Samson is called to be a judge from before his birth, and he's also designated as a Nazirite, a special individual. Judges 13:5 states, "No razor shall touch his head, for the boy is to be a Nazirite for God from the womb." According to the rules for Nazirites set forth in the book of Numbers, being a Nazirite would have also obliged Samson to abstain from wine and other alcohol as well as avoid contact with dead bodies—all of which Samson flaunts.

The rabbis can't decide if Samson is good or bad because of his flaunting of the Nazirite rules. For instance, chapter 15 finds him acquiring strength from something unclean that he's not even supposed to touch: the fresh jawbone of a donkey, which he uses as a weapon to kill 1,000 Philistines.

In chapter 16, Samson has gone down into Philistia to find women. First, he finds a prostitute, foils an ambush, and carries away the great posts of the city gate all the way to Hebron, 37 miles away. Verse 4 finds him in a big wine-producing region, finally meeting Delilah.

Delilah cajoles him into revealing the source of his strength. With every answer he gives, she attempts to remove his strength and have him captured. In the usual reading of this story, he finally admits it is his long hair. She cuts off his hair. His strength is gone, and the Philistines overpower him and take him away.

However, that's not quite what the story says. Samson doesn't seem to think that cutting his hair will cause him to lose his strength any more than any of Delilah's previous actions did.

The issue is not that the strength was in his hair. It was no more in his hair than it was in any of the other lies he told to Delilah. But he assumed that God would continue to overlook his foolishness, and God has finally had enough.

LECTURE 11 | THE BOOK OF JUDGES

Samson and Delilah, José Echenagusia Errazquin

Samson is blinded, and months later, he is brought before the lords of the Philistines. He is made to stand between two columns, and he finally prays to God. This is only the second time he has ever prayed: "Lord God, remember me, strengthen me, only this once, that I may avenge myself on the Philistines at one blow for my eyes."

Samson is merely after vengeance for his eyes. God, however, gives him the strength to bring the temple down on his own head, "killing more in his death than he had in his lifetime."

God is here responding to the Philistine praise of their own god in verse 24: "Our god has delivered our enemy into our power." Samson's renewed strength, the destruction of the Philistine temple, and the deaths he inflicts are God's message for the Philistines and the Philistine god.

Conclusion

The remaining chapters bring the book of Judges to a tragic finale. A judge was supposed to reform religious practice, correct unethical behavior, and then bring military independence. However, the ending tragically shows first religious chaos in chapters 17 and 18, then moral depravity in chapter 19, and finally military self-destruction in chapter 20.

The book concludes in chapter 21, verse 25, with the editorial comment: "In those days there was no king in Israel; everyone did what was right in their own eyes." Without leadership, even gross violations of idolatry were permitted, and without direction, even misplaced justice brings about the near-annihilation of the tribe.

There is no happy ending to the book of Judges, only a decline into idolatry, immorality, and violence. The book does not complete Israel's conquest of Canaan. Instead, it depicts the people of Israel becoming worse than the Canaanites.

Questions to Consider

- Why does Samson often look like a mythological hero?
- Why is there so much violence against children in the book of Judges?

Suggested Reading

Miller, *Chieftains of the Highland Clans.*

Webb, *The Book of Judges.*

THE BOOKS OF SAMUEL

LECTURE 12

This lecture looks at the books 1 and 2 Samuel and introduces the kings Saul, David, and Solomon. Historically speaking, these two books trace the career of Samuel—the last in a series of charismatic leaders, or judges, of the Old Testament.

Background on Samuel

Though Samuel is the last judge, he is not a very good example of a typical prophet, because he's also a priest, judge, and kingmaker. He is associated with a curious early prophetic institution: the prophetic bands. These were ecstatic groups of individuals who seem to go into trances brought on by God. Much of the time when they appear, there is a father-guardian who seems to oversee them. Samuel plays this role.

But then this kind of ecstatic prophecy seems to die out. The theme that carries through is the sense of self-transcendence behind prophecy: What comes out of the prophet's mouth is from God, not the prophet.

As Samuel nears death, the Israelites wonder how they'll be led in the future. In 1 Samuel 8:1, it is revealed "In his old age, Samuel appointed his sons judges over Israel." However, they "did not follow his example." Instead, they accepted bribes and perverted justice. The elders of Israel in turn demanded that Samuel appoint a king "like all the nations."

Samuel Anointed Saul as King

LECTURE 12 | THE BOOKS OF SAMUEL

Verse 4 states, "Therefore, all the elders of Israel assembled and went to Samuel…and said to him, 'Now that you are old and your sons do not follow your example, appoint a king over us like all the nations to rule us.'"

Monarchy

Under the covenant or agreement the Israelites had entered into with God at Mount Sinai, Yahweh was Israel's true king. Having a king "like the other nations" is a rejection of that. However, God gives in and tells Samuel to appoint a king.

This is the moment when monarchy appears in Israel. Every other ancient people considered monarchy to be the inherent system of the universe. In Israel, however, monarchy originates at a defined point in time. It's not human society's default position. That's a statement of political philosophy.

Furthermore, the decision to move to monarchy has been initiated by the people. As political theorists and philosophers from Thomas Jefferson to John Locke would say, government derives from the mandate of the people. This is a radical belief. It is possible draw a direct line from this biblical statement to the period of the Enlightenment and, from there, to the political theories that went into the birth of the United States.

In chapter 8, Samuel tells the people that monarchs are dangerous and that they "will cry out because of the king you have chosen, but the Lord will not answer you on that day." Samuel is making the people understand that it is as an inherently unjust form of government.

Saul and David

The first king that Samuel selects is Saul. Saul is in many ways a dumb brute, and he is handicapped by the fact that Samuel does not retire after making him king. Instead, Samuel expects Saul to continue to follow his will. Saul never really controls much more than the tribe of Benjamin.

Eventually, Saul's future successor David enters the picture. As soon as Saul realizes David is gaining in popularity and seeks to kill him, David joins the enemy, becoming a Philistine. He took "600 soldiers and went over to Achish king of Gath."

When the Philistines go to war with Israel, David is ready to join up. However, the Philistines are not yet completely comfortable with David or his loyalties, and they don't take him along. Still, the Philistines defeat Saul, who dies at his own hand.

Now left to take over Israel himself, David consolidates his rule and wipes out the remainder of Saul's family. He eventually manages to take the city of Jerusalem, making it his capital.

Bathsheba

David remains brutal throughout his reign, exemplified by the famous episode with Bathsheba, the wife of a Hittite named Uriah, who is off at war. One evening, as depicted in 2 Samuel 11, David sees Bathsheba bathing and sends people to take her. Though her present-day reputation is that of a seductress, the truth is far from it; Bathsheba is, if anything, a victim of rape.

She becomes pregnant. David sends for Uriah from the frontlines, brings him home, gets him drunk, and invites him to return home where he can be with his wife. David's goal is to give everyone the impression—including the husband himself—that the child will be his.

King David Handing the Letter to Uriah, Pieter Lastman, 1611.

LECTURE 12 | THE BOOKS OF SAMUEL

Uriah sleeps on David's doorstep instead. David's convenient solution fails. He is forced to compound his rape with the crime of murder. He arranges for Uriah to be placed at the front line of the war, and he has the rest of the army withdraw, leaving Uriah exposed. After Uriah is killed, verse 26 states David sends for Bathsheba and brings her into his house. She has no choice, and "in the sight of the Lord what David has done was evil."

This is followed by the arrival of the prophet Nathan. Nathan is not one of the ecstatic band prophets. However, he is a spokesman for God to David and later to David's son and successor Solomon.

God has something to say to David here about the Bathsheba episode. Nathan makes up a parable about a poor man whose wealthy neighbor steals his only lamb. When David proclaims the man is worthy of death, Nathan famously says, "You are the man!"

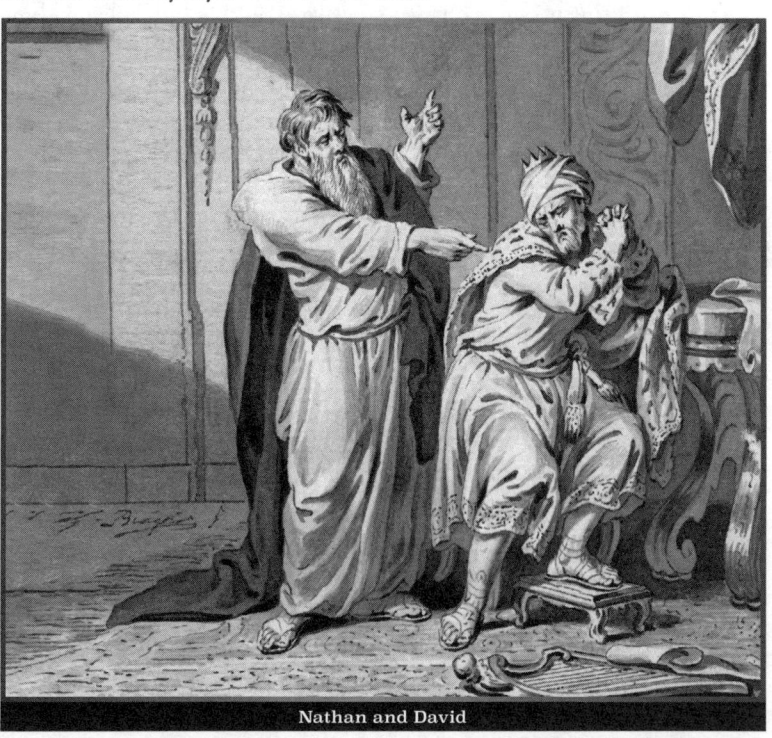

Nathan and David

David's child by Bathsheba dies. But that's only the beginning. The terrible collision of David's avarice, lust, royal privilege, and murder leads to more sexual violence and family assassination that mark the rest of David's reign. David never truly changes his ways.

Solomon

Solomon succeeds David, and Solomon's reign is comparatively peaceful. He's also famous for constructing what is now known as Solomon's Temple, the first temple to Israel's God in Jerusalem. Today, no archaeological remains survive. (Visible in Jerusalem today are remnants of the Second Temple, constructed in the time of Ezra and Nehemiah in the 5th century BCE and thoroughly renovated by Herod the Great in the 1st century CE.)

From the Bible's description of Solomon's Temple, it was a three-part structure consisting of outer courts, a sanctuary, and a holy of holies within. Its floor plan is identical to any temple from ancient Syria or Phoenicia.

However, in the back, where the statue of the god would otherwise be, Solomon's Temple had the Ark of the Covenant. The Ark was a large, gold-plated wooden chest. Inside were the two stone tablets Moses received from God.

LECTURE 12 | THE BOOKS OF SAMUEL

This signifies that the central focus of Israel's worship is a text, not an image. In other words, whereas Greeks or Phoenicians would pray oriented toward a statue of Zeus or Athena or Astarte, Israel focused its attention on a document, the agreement attesting to their relationship with God.

Questions to Consider

- ✡ Is David a great hero or a traitor? Which tradition is more important for the Old Testament, and why?
- ✡ Does the Old Testament think monarchy is good or bad?

Suggested Reading

Halpern, *David's Secret Demons*.

Houston, *Justice*.

QUIZ 2

1. *Decalogue* means:
a. 10 fingers
b. 10 plagues
c. 10 words
d. 10 commandments

2. "You shall not hew steps leading up to my altar" because:
a. Stone is sacred to God.
b. The priestly vestments were too tight fitting.
c. There was no underwear in antiquity.
d. The animal offerings would escape

3. Which of the following is kosher?
a. crawdads
b. squirrel
c. crickets
d. shark meat

4. Deuteronomistic theology is basically:
a. Do good, receive good.
b. If you make sacrifices, your injustice won't matter.
c. Life is vanity of vanities.

QUIZ 2

5. When Jephthah promised to sacrifice the first thing to come out of his house upon his homecoming, he probably expected:

a. his daughter
b. his wife
c. a sheep
d. the neighbor

6. Which of the following does King David not do?

a. commit adultery
b. join the enemy
c. worship Baal
d. have his officer murdered

Answers: 1.(c); 2.(c); 3.(c); 4.(a); 5.(a); 6.(c)

THE BOOKS OF KINGS
LECTURE 13

The Old Testament books of First and Second Kings tell the history of Israel from the time of King Solomon in the 10th century BCE up until the destruction of the Israelite kingdoms of Israel and Judah in the late 8th and early 6th centuries. These books also introduce us to the position of prophet. This lecture is devoted to looking at prophecy in Israel and specifically how prophecy is treated in the books of Kings.

Background on the Books of Kings

The books of Kings are considered by scholars to be part of the Deuteronomistic History, a comprehensive account running from Joshua through Kings that wasn't written to tell ancient Israelites about the past so much as to provide them with moral lessons to live by. Specifically, these books were designed to show that when God's law is followed, there is prosperity, and when the law is broken, there is disaster.

LECTURE 13 | THE BOOKS OF KINGS

An example of this occurs early in the book of 1 Kings. The Israelite kingdom that had been ruled by David and Solomon is split into a divided monarchy, with the northern kingdom known as Israel and the smaller southern kingdom known as Judah.

Judah is home to Jerusalem, and preserves the monarchy in the house of David. In contrast, the northern kingdom goes through multiple different dynasties.

Chapter 12 of 1 Kings provides a theological explanation of why this happens. Northern tribes approach Solomon's son, Rehoboam, and they ask how harsh a king he will be compared to his father. Ignoring the advice of his elders—and following the counsel of some of his young friends—Rehoboam says he will be extremely harsh and put northern tribes disproportionately into conscripted labor.

The northerners decide not to follow the house of David in the person of Rehoboam. Rehoboam rules over the Israelites in the towns of Judah, while the northern tribes form a kingdom with the name Israel under a king named Jeroboam.

The northern kingdom became much more prosperous, but prosperity primarily favored the rich. Class distinctions became much greater in the northern kingdom than in the southern. Eventually, the Israelite royal dynasty intermarries with Phoenicians.

The Israelite king Ahab marries the infamous Jezebel, and the Phoenician religion is imported into Israel. Prosperity and international exposure also meant that the northern kingdom was at war more often than—and conquered long before—the southern kingdom of Judah.

Israelite Prophecy

A prophet is a spokesperson for God regarding the present, not primarily a foreteller of the future. God doesn't possess the prophet so much as inspire their words. The prophet's role is to be the conscience of the nation: calling people back to fidelity to their covenant with God. Specifically, the prophet focuses on those parts of the covenant that deal with three areas.

The first is monotheism, the belief in one god. The threat to this is local non-Israelite fertility gods and also—more stubbornly—non-normative types of Yahweh worship.

The second area of the prophets' concern is covenant morality, especially social justice. The third area that prophets spend their attention on is God's will in current events.

God's position on current events is a moving target. In one century, the prophet Isaiah tells the king not to surrender to the besieging army, because God will defend his people. In the next century, the prophet Jeremiah tells the king to surrender to the besieging army, because God has chosen to punish us. The situation has changed, so the message is different.

Elijah

Elijah is a prominent prophet in the books of Kings. A long oral tradition was gathered into documents about Elijah, and those eventually were worked into 1 Kings, chapters 17 through 19. Early on, Elijah is instructed by God where to flee during a drought. Elijah follows these instructions and is safe.

Eventually, the word of the Lord comes to Elijah and tells him to go to Phoenicia. When he's there, he meets a widow and her son who are about to starve to death during a drought. Elijah asks for water and bread.

The widow doesn't want to share her meager resources. Nevertheless, Elijah says to trust him and feed him, and that they won't starve. Miraculously their flour and oil last until the drought ends.

Next, the boy becomes sick, and his mother appeals to Elijah, who cries "out to the Lord." In verse 22, the Lord listens to the prayer of Elijah, and the boy is healed.

To summarize: When Elijah listens to God's word, he lives. When the woman listens to Elijah's word, she lives. God listens to Elijah's word, and the boy lives. This begs the question: Will Ahab listen?

LECTURE 13 | THE BOOKS OF KINGS

Elijah and the widow

The Contest

In chapter 18, Elijah confronts Ahab and the priests and prophets of the god Baal. He proposes a contest. The background context is this: Ahab's marriage to a Phoenician queen introduces a foreign religion. Ahab and Jezebel attempt to establish an absolute monarchy, and importing the worship of the fertility god Baal is part of that.

As king and queen, Ahab and Jezebel assume the role of Baal's chief priests. Baal is also a storm god, and in this part of the Middle East, fertility is tied to rain. The contest, which takes place on Mount Carmel, is about whether the storm god can bring lightning or not. The contest will show how Yahweh—the Hebrew God—alone has power, while Baal, the Phoenician god—is impotent. The point is to call the people back to their original obligations under the covenant with God.

Elijah convenes a contest in which both sets of prophets will arrange a sacrifice to see which god can bring down fire or strike the offering—a bull—with lightning. The prophets of Baal call upon their god to strike the bull, but nothing happens. However, eventually "fire from the Lord" consumes the offering. Elijah then slaughters the prophets of Baal. A problem remains: Ahab and Jezebel, who threatens him. Frightened for his life, Elijah flees into the desert.

The Fallout

Chapter 19 presents an unflattering picture of Elijah. He continues to flee, walking "for 40 days and 40 nights as far as the Mountain of God, Horeb." He spends the night in a cave here. Horeb is Mount Sinai, where Moses received the Law from God during the Exodus. The cave is the same cave where God appeared before Moses in the book of Exodus. In many ways, Elijah is a new Moses, as he stands where Moses did.

God asks Elijah why he is there. Elijah says he is "moved by the zeal for the Lord," but blames the Israelite people—rather than Ahab and Jezebel—for abandoning their covenant.

Elijah also claims "I alone am left." However, in verse 18, it is revealed that there are 7,000 others. In no other place of the Old Testament do so many prophets appear in such a short space. Elijah is hardly alone.

In verse 11, God calls Elijah to "Stand on the mountain before the Lord." However, Elijah won't come out until the end of verse 13. Then comes this passage:

> The Lord passed by. There was a great and mighty wind splitting mountains and shattering rocks by the power of the Lord. The Lord was not in the wind. And after the wind, an earthquake. The Lord was not in the earthquake. And after the earthquake, fire. The Lord was not in the fire. And after the fire, a still small voice. When Elijah heard it, he wrapped his mantle about his face and went out and stood at the entrance of the cave.

LECTURE 13 | THE BOOKS OF KINGS

The gale, earthquake, and fire are ways that God appears in other parts of the Old Testament. The point is not that God is never in such things. Additionally, the climax is not the still small voice.

God immediately says: "Why are you here, Elijah?" And Elijah answers: "I am moved by the zeal for the Lord." In other words, Elijah is repeating himself, as if to say he is done.

God tells him to go back the way he came, and when he gets there, to anoint "Hazael as king of Aram, anoint Jehu … as king of Israel, and Elisha … to succeed you as prophet." God also says, "Whoever escapes the sword of Hazael shall be slain by Jehu. Whoever escapes the sword of Jehu shall be slain by Elisha."

However, Elijah doesn't end up doing any of this. Instead, the only thing he does is anoint Elisha as his successor. God is telling Elijah to stop whining, but also signaling that he can be replaced.

The Decline

The book of 2 Kings records the decline of the northern kingdom that Elijah sets in motion. Israel will eventually fall to the rising empire of Assyria. The Assyrian king Sargon II will finish it off in 702 BCE.

Additionally, 2 Kings 17 and 18 describe how the Assyrians deport the inhabitants to other parts of their empire. Those deportees become the so-called Ten Lost Tribes. The deported Israelites simply assimilated into Assyrian society.

LECTURE 13 | THE BOOKS OF KINGS

The Assyrians imported foreigners into Israel, and they came to worship Yahweh while preserving some of their foreign religions. These are the people that come to be known as Samaritans.

Assyria had also invaded the southern kingdom of Judah. The Assyrian leader Sennacherib campaigned against Judah's King Hezekiah, and five different accounts in Assyrian records describe the invasion. Forty-six Judean cities were besieged, and many captives were taken.

Assyrian sources say Sennacherib went home without conquering Jerusalem but that Hezekiah sent a huge tribute. Chapters 18 and 19 of 2 Kings say that God struck the besieging army dead, just as Isaiah had prophesied he would to defend Jerusalem. In fact, part of the explanation for the Assyrian retreat was the approach of an Egyptian army under the leadership of the ruling Ethiopian dynasty, a combined Egyptian-Ethiopian army that the Assyrians did not want to confront.

However, Judah was left badly devastated. The Assyrian empire fell in 612, but Judah's days were numbered. The Babylonian Empire rose in 605 under the king Nebuchadnezzar, and Judah falls under its sway in 2 Kings 24.

Rebellion and Hope

Judah was determined to be independent. Her last kings—the last kings of the house of David—rebelled against Babylon. In 2 Kings 24:10, 597 BCE, Jerusalem falls, and many people are taken captive to Babylon. According to 2 Kings, the king, Jehoiachin, was deported and provided for in Babylon, as Babylonian records confirm. The Babylonians put a new king in place.

That king, Zedekiah, again foolishly revolts. As 2 Kings 25 recounts, the city of Jerusalem falls to Nebuchadnezzar in July of 586. The temple is demolished, and its goods are taken to Babylon. Zedekiah's eyes are put out, and he's taken in chains to Babylon, ending the reign of the house of David. The nobles, merchants, and officers of Judah go into exile in Babylon.

In the last verses of this book, hope is offered in the form of a somewhat forgotten character: King Jehoiachin, exiled back in 597 BCE. The book of 2 Kings 25:27–30 says that in his 36th year of exile:

> [The] King …of Babylon, in the year he became king, pardoned King Jehoiachin of Judah and released him from prison. He treated him with kindness and gave him a throne above those of other kings who were with him in Babylon. So Jehoiachin removed his prison garments, and for the rest of his life always ate at the king's table.

In other words, the royal family was still alive. There's hope that the line of David will continue and perhaps Israel could return from exile. God's promise to David that his dynasty will always rule over Jerusalem—seemingly thrown to the wind by the fall of the kingdom—may prove true, after all.

Questions to Consider

- In the end, do the books of Kings look favorably upon Elijah?
- Was the conquest of Judah inevitable, or were its kings just foolish to rebel?

Suggested Reading

Heller, *Characters of Elijah and Elisha and the Deuteronomic Evaluation of Prophecy.*

Heschel, *The Prophets.*

BIBLICAL SHORT STORIES: RUTH AND ESTHER

LECTURE 14

This lecture looks at a specific genre of books in the Old Testament: short stories. Before that, the lecture provides some historical background.

An Exile

A large portion of the population of Judah was deported to Babylon after the conquest of Jerusalem by Nebuchadnezzar, the king of Babylon. The Jews remained in Babylon for roughly the next 50 years, until 539 BCE. (Many stayed much longer.) They thrived as a minority group in a larger population. Additionally, the Babylonian captivity saw the forging of the Jewish religion.

The Exile

The central feature of Israelite religion prior to the exile was sacrifice of animals in the temple in Jerusalem. No temple would be built in Babylon. Still, a place where Jews gather to hear the scriptures, pray, and sing is called a synagogue. It is in the Babylonian exile that the word *synagogue* first appears, mentioned in the book of Ezekiel. Unfortunately, no synagogues have ever been found in ancient Iraq from this period, so it is impossible to be certain about this topic.

LECTURE 14 | BIBLICAL SHORT STORIES: RUTH AND ESTHER

Although many of the festivals of the Jewish calendar would become impossible without the temple, it was certainly possible to keep the Sabbath. Kosher diet laws could be maintained and circumcision preserved. All of these things, in fact, became more important in exile, so the community could distinguish itself from its neighbors.

The letters used for the Hebrew language for the past two millennia are Aramaic letters, adopted during the Babylonian exile. The lingua franca of the Babylonian empire, Aramaic, became the spoken language of the Jews as well.

After the Exile

In 539 BCE, the Persian king Cyrus conquered the Babylonian Empire. Part of Cyrus's policy to ensure loyalty was to allow multiple peoples whom the Babylonians had exiled to return home, the Jews among them. However, the restored Jewish community in Judah was by no means independent, nor would it be for centuries.

It was a province of the Persian Empire until the late 4th century BCE, when it became a province of Alexander the Great's empire. Independence for the Jews was never an option. They were a small, powerless people. That's important for understanding the literature we're about to read.

Postexilic Stories

A new genre emerged in the postexilic period: short stories, or totally independent books that are single brief plots. Several of them are accepted as canonical scripture by Catholics and Eastern Orthodox Christians but not by Protestants or Jews.

There is a predominance of women in this genre. Three of the books have women as the main character: Ruth, Esther, and Judith. They are women doubly at risk. Ruth is both a woman and a foreigner. Esther is a woman and an orphan. Judith is a woman and a widow. In the narratives of these three books, traditionally male values fail.

The Book of Ruth

In Judaism's ordering of the books of the Bible, the book of Ruth is placed at the very end with the other short stories. In the Christian Bible, the book of Ruth is earlier, between Judges and 1 Samuel because that's the time setting for the narrative. Ruth 1:1 says, "In the days when the judges ruled." That's the narrative setting for this short story.

In the story, the character Ruth is repeatedly referred to as "Ruth the Moabite." There is no escaping her despised foreign identity. It's not clear how other characters know she's Moabite, but there is no way to avoid it regardless.

The twists and turns of the story deliver a twofold message: On the one hand, when you are weak and traditional power is not available to you, then loyalty and your own wits can save you. The second message is about foreigners and perhaps about intermarriage. This is a book against segregation; it sees no value in purity of blood.

Ruth in Boaz's Field, Julius Schnorr von Carolsfeld, 1828

LECTURE 14 | BIBLICAL SHORT STORIES: RUTH AND ESTHER

The Book of Esther

The book of Esther is set in the Persian Empire, and portrays it fairly accurately, albeit comically. The background is that Persian rule was always considered by the Jews to be positive. Persia was good. Persians did not commit atrocities; they restored the exiles and the temple. There were no Jewish rebellions against the Persians.

The Persian king, Ahasuerus, is made out to be a joke. Ahasuerus is obsessed with honor and with appearing generous, with the result that anyone's will can become law.

An example of this occurs in Esther 1:16–21, where the officer Memuchan turns a marital spat into a national crisis and then tells the king how to deal with it. Queen Vashti refuses to appear when summoned. Memuchan says this is a disaster for the entire nation, and then he tells the king exactly what edict to pass.

Similarly, the king's officer, Haman, manufactures a dilemma and proposes the solution: a genocide of the Jews. The king immediately signs it into law and then sits down to dinner as if nothing is unusual.

Queen Vashti

Later, Ahasuerus says he cannot rescind the law he made for Haman, although he had forgotten that it was he who initiated the genocide in the first place. However, he immediately grants his new Jewish queen Esther and her uncle Mordechai royal authority: "Do whatever you want to defend the Jews."

Haman has incited the king to a type of Judeophobia because they "want to follow their own Torah law." However, the real reason is Haman's anger at Mordechai. Mordechai did not bow when he passed by.

A background factor of this situation is that the king has remarried Mordechai's niece, the Jewish queen Esther. It is Esther who will save the day by revealing to the king that she is Jewish and that Haman's law would exterminate her and her people.

This is what provokes the king to allow her and Mordechai to do whatever they need to defend the Jewish people. The result is a happy ending for the saved Jews, but it reads rather uncomfortably, as they massacre many Persians.

Conclusion

Some biblical scholars focus on the final chapters and see the entire book of Esther as presenting a rabid Jewish hatred of gentiles. This is a misreading. For example, the book does not blame all gentiles. Chapter 9 says in the first three verses that a number of the Persians supported the Jews. Mordechai's coworkers knew all along that he was Jewish and never had a problem with it. There is certainly no issue with intermarriage, because it is Esther's marriage to a gentile that saves her people.

This doesn't mean that one can't be a little uncomfortable with Jews' actions in chapter 9. Even Jewish theologians like the Israeli Shalom Ben-Chorin have been clear to condemn it. However, the Persians were hardly defenseless victims after Mordechai's edict. According to 8:11, Ahasuerus "permitted the Jews of every city to assemble and fight for their lives." It goes on to say, "If any people attacks them, they may destroy massacre and exterminate the armed bands that attacked them."

Jews in the postexilic period never had the opportunity for any armed action like that depicted in the ending of the book of Esther. The real message of the book is clear if Esther stands for Israel. It's fine to intermarry; it's fine to work in the Persian government, as Mordechai does. One can be an integral part of the larger gentile society and still keep his or her Jewishness.

LECTURE 14 | BIBLICAL SHORT STORIES: RUTH AND ESTHER

Esther succeeds when she remembers she's Jewish and when she admits it at the right time. She succeeds by her wits, just as Ruth does. The postexilic Jews couldn't depend on the Persian government, and the story of Esther shows that political power itself is never going to be of much use in their favor. However, there are other ways—which the Israelites seem to have thought of as feminine ways—to remain true to God and preserve the Jewish people.

Questions to Consider

- Some scholars have described Ahasuerus's rejected queen, Vashti, as just as foreign as Esther merely by being a woman in a man's world. What do you think?

- Is the book of Ruth a positive or negative portrait of women and foreigners?

Suggested Reading

Bellis, *Helpmates, Harlots, and Heroes*.

Fox, *Character and Ideology in the Book of Esther*.

AMOS, PROPHET OF JUSTICE

LECTURE 15

This lecture focuses on the prophet Amos. He personifies the focus on social justice that is central to all of the Hebrew prophets of the Old Testament. In a sense, Amos is the earliest prophet for whom we have a separate book.

Background on the Book of Amos

The prophets were primarily oral proclaimers, and it fell to other people to collect and edit their works. Amos is set apart in comparison to prophets like Elijah and Elisha because there are collections of the prophet's sayings in a discrete book as opposed to merely stories about the prophet.

LECTURE 15 | AMOS, PROPHET OF JUSTICE

We're told that Amos "prophesies against" the northern kingdom Israel, and the dates that are described fall somewhere between 786 and 746 BCE. That was a time of great prosperity for the northern kingdom. Unfortunately, it was both a prosperous and an intensely stratified society.

The words of Amos were collected orally, passed down through the generations by word-of-mouth, and eventually put into writing. It is likely that the stories of Amos were assembled into the form that we have during the Babylonian exile, around 540 BCE.

Themes of the Book of Amos

There are two main themes to the book of Amos. He is often called the prophet of righteousness. The word meaning "righteousness" in Hebrew is *tzedakah*. In modern Hebrew, *tzedakah* means "charity." However, in the Old Testament, *tzedakah* means "right covenant relationships." It's not about being righteous in the sense of not sinning. It means every Israelite is in the right covenant relationship with every other Israelite and with God.

Amos fundamentally sees *tzedakah* as about economics. There are more words meaning "poor" in the book of Amos than anywhere else in the Bible. Amos's basic thesis is this: Israel's lack of *tzedakah*, its lack of right covenant relationship, is best seen in the treatment of the poor. For instance, if the judges are taking bribes, a rich person can get justice from an unjust judge. A poor person cannot.

The book of Amos has a second theme, which can be framed in this way: There is no cultic security blanket. The existence of a cultic security blanket would mean that God will pay no attention to a person's unjust deeds as long as the person continues the rituals of worship. Amos is perhaps the first prophet to emphasize that there is no cultic security blanket.

Amos's Style

The prophets are oral proclaimers and are very skilled at rhetoric; they have a way of speaking poetically. Their speeches, when read in Hebrew, are filled with puns and rhythm, and they also know how to draw a crowd. In Amos 1:3, there is a repeated pattern that turns into a crowd chant: "Thus says the Lord for three transgressions of Damascus, and for four, I will not revoke it: because they thrashed Gilead with threshing boards of iron. I will send down fire upon Bit-Hazael."

Each denunciation of a different enemy begins for three transgressions and for four. Using this pattern, Amos first denounces Damascus. Israel, the northern kingdom, was perpetually at war with Damascus.

The second enemy Amos denounces is the Philistines. Then, he goes after the Phoenicians, and then Edom. It seems that a crowd is continually growing around Amos, and he next denounces the Ammonites, Moab, and Judah.

LECTURE 15 | AMOS, PROPHET OF JUSTICE

The Finale of Amos's Speech

There is a distinct difference in the rhetoric against Judah. Judah is not condemned for war crimes. They are condemned for rejecting the law of God. This opens the door for the start of the grand finale in verse 6: "For three transgressions of Israel, and for four, I will not revoke the punishment, because they sell the righteous for silver and the needy for a pair of sandals."

Israel is called out for several crimes, and they're all against the poor. The line regarding sandals is about debt slavery. Then, Amos 2:7 decries the violation of a law that prohibits a woman from being a concubine for the whole house. If she is the concubine for the son, the father must treat her as a daughter.

The next verse highlights another problem: "They reclined by every altar on garments taken in pledge." In Amos 2:8, they are accused of sleeping on garments taken in pledge, and keeping the pledge garments overnight is forbidden. The fact that they're sleeping in the temple of God shows the hypocrisy of these abuses.

The Woes

In a section of the middle of the book, Amos has three woes. One starts in 5:7, another in 5:18, and then in 6:1. The middle of those is the structural center of the book. Amos 5:18 reads, "Woe to you who desire the day of the Lord." This is the earliest reference we have to the day of the Lord—or end of time—anywhere in the Bible. The passage doesn't introduce the concept of the end of the world. Instead, it's criticizing people who long for it.

Why would someone long for the end of the world? Such people are looking forward to God coming in glory and conquering all of their enemies. Amos cuts off this security blanket by pointing out the day of the Lord will involve judgment. Later, Amos denounces the hypocrisy of thinking that one can treat the poor horribly, but make animal sacrifices and be fine.

The End of the Book of Amos

Amos does offer some hope. Some think the verses at the end of the book are a late addition put in by Jews in exile in Babylon, and that Amos himself didn't offer any hope. However, these verses are consistent with the rest of the message of Amos. For instance, chapter 9, verse 13 reads:

> Behold, the days are coming, declares the Lord, when the plowman shall overtake the reaper, and the treader of grapes him who sows the seed. The mountains shall drip sweet wine and the hills shall flow with it. ... I will plant them on their land, and they shall never again be uprooted.

This is consistent with Amos's vision that paradise is bucolic. The blessings are the prosperity of plowing, reaping, wine, harvests and gardens. The blessings are not ivory, musical instruments, or veal. There is a distinct contrast between the values of Israel's consumerists and God's rural agricultural paradise that is consistent with what Amos thinks is important in life throughout the book. There is hope—although God's hope might not be what the people expect.

Questions to Consider

✡ Did Amos and similar prophets want to end poverty in ancient Israel?

✡ Does Amos place any value on sacrifice and other rituals?

Suggested Reading

Eidevall, *Amos*.

Ho, *Ṣedeq and Ṣedaqah in the Hebrew Bible*.

THE PROPHET ISAIAH IN THREE MOVEMENTS
LECTURE 16

The book of Isaiah has three distinct movements. Each one has a specific historical context. The book as a whole is one piece, intentionally woven together around 520 BCE. This lecture gives an overview of the book's contents.

An Important Time and the First Movement

The book of Isaiah puts the prophet in Jerusalem at an important time. He's there when the Assyrian Empire has conquered the northern kingdom of Israel. The Assyrians also overran most of the kingdom of Judah. King Hezekiah and the city of Jerusalem survived, and Isaiah is there for that event, as the book of Kings describes. This is roughly 720 to 700 BCE. Isaiah was in a high enough position to interact regularly with the king.

UNDERSTANDING THE OLD TESTAMENT

King Hezekiah and Isaiah

Early in the book, Isaiah's denunciations are primarily about social injustice. For instance, in chapter 5, he calls out individual owners gaining more and more land. Isaiah also calls out the masses, who didn't know the law properly, and who didn't know who God was so that they could emulate him. Isaiah says the punishment for such crimes will be exile.

The book of Isaiah is not all bad news. An important notion emerges in Israelite religion in the early part of the book: the concept of the Messiah.

LECTURE 16 | THE PROPHET ISAIAH IN THREE MOVEMENTS

The Second Movement

Beginning in the 12th century CE, rabbis noted that something happens after Isaiah 39: The prophet Isaiah is no longer mentioned, and the entire context seems to have changed. Since 1775, biblical scholars have proposed that Isaiah chapters 40 to 55 are the work of an author later than Isaiah of Jerusalem, the product of the Babylonian exile in the 6th century BCE.

The audience's situation has changed because the enemy of the Jewish people is not Assyria. It is Babylon. The environment of the people has changed because they're living in Babylon, not Jerusalem. Additionally, the vocabulary is different. The theology is different as well: The overall message of Isaiah 40 to 55 is comfort and a promise of restoration.

One of the main themes of this section is that Israel's redemption will come at the hands of Persia. The prophet is under no illusion that the Persian king Cyrus acknowledges God or believes Yahweh has granted him victory. But the Israelites are assured that behind the scenes, Cyrus's conquest of Babylon is God's doing.

Another theme in this section of Isaiah is a literary character known as the suffering servant, who is presented in a series of so-called servant songs. The term was coined in the 1920s by the German scholar Bernhard Duhm, who identified the servant songs.

In the New Testament, Christianity identified the suffering servant as Jesus. That's because in Isaiah, God accepts the servant's suffering and death as reparation, while, on the other hand, the frail, obedient servant of the Lord ends up elevated to an almost divine status. However, another reading is that the servant is Israel. Israel suffers. God accepts its suffering as reparation and extends God's salvation to the Gentile nations.

The Third Movement

The third and final movement of the book of Isaiah is the section after chapter 55. Scholars have come to date this to a later period when the people of Israel—having returned from the exile in Babylon—resumed life as a free people in the land of their ancestors and rebuilt Jerusalem. The name Isaiah is not found in these chapters.

The setting of these chapters is Jerusalem, and Jerusalem is in ruins, not much rebuilt. The salvation promised is for a small remnant, not for the whole nation. The situation, however, is tense and divisive, unlike that in chapters 40 to 55. Also, unlike all of the earlier chapters of Isaiah, observance of the Sabbath becomes important.

Isaiah 58 gives a description of people who are much more pious than in the opening chapters of Isaiah. But there's a problem: Israel's values are still distorted. People are trying to cover up injustices with fasting, praying, and hearing righteous ordinances, which are synagogue practices.

Another important feature of this section of Isaiah is a new universalism: an outgrowth of salvation to the nations. This can be viewed as a prediction that foreigners will also be included in the highest form of worship to the one God.

Questions to Consider

✡ What does it help to read the parts of Isaiah against three distinct historical settings?

✡ What would King Cyrus have thought of Isaiah if he had read it?

Suggested Reading

Cook, *Conversations with Scripture: 2 Isaiah*.

Heskett, *Messianism within the Scriptural Scroll of Isaiah*.

JEREMIAH, PERSECUTED PROPHET
LECTURE 17

In the book of Jeremiah, we see Jeremiah being persecuted more than any other prophet. He's made a laughingstock. He's thrown into a cistern—a water-storage tank—in an attempted assassination. Outwardly, he appears stubborn as a mule. But we get a glimpse into his thoughts and see that he is in turmoil: He questions whether he really wants to be a prophet.

Background on the Book of Jeremiah

Jeremiah's book places him at the end of Judah's history. He's in Jerusalem when it's conquered in 586 BCE by the Babylonians. As with the other prophets, much of the Jeremiah's prophecy was delivered orally, collected, and assembled. In this case, we know the name of his scribe: Baruch. A good guess would be that the final assembly, or at least most of it, took place around 530 BCE.

There are two overarching themes to the book of Jeremiah. The American biblical scholar Walter Brueggemann calls these two themes "to pluck up and tear down" and "to build and to plant."

The First Message

The first message is to tear down and to uproot. God has chosen to give the Jews to Babylon as punishment for their centuries of disobedience to him. The Jews' best option is to surrender to the Babylonians.

Eventually in the book, King Josiah, the righteous king—who reigned from about 641 BCE to about 610 BCE— has died. He was succeeded for a couple of days by his son, Shalum.

The Egyptians took Shalum as a prisoner and replaced him on the throne with another of Josiah's sons, Jehoiakim. Jehoiakim is and will remain an Egyptian puppet. The Egyptian pharaoh commands tribute, and Jehoiakim—instead of paying it out of his royal coffers—takes it as a tax from the people. At the same time, Jehoiakim also built a new palace. Jeremiah cries out about the combination of taxing the people to pay Egypt while enhancing his own luxury.

Jehoiakim Burns the Word of God; as in Jeremiah

LECTURE 17 | JEREMIAH, PERSECUTED PROPHET

After Jehoiakim

When Jehoiakim died, he was succeeded by other anti-Babylonian kings. The first was Jehoiachin, who reigned for three months in the year 597. From that short period, we have Jeremiah's powerful temple sermon in chapter 7, which was against empty, false worship as well as idolatry, injustice, and why empty rituals don't make up for those sins.

This occurred only a generation after a thorough reform undertaken by King Josiah, who cleaned all sorts of idolatrous installations out of the temple. It appears that Josiah's reform produced only superficial results.

The Confessions of Jeremiah

This lecture now turns to what the scholar Walter Baumgartner identified as the confessions of Jeremiah. These are insights into Jeremiah that he reveals when he is alone with God. There are six of them. Each has four parts: an invocation of God, quotation of the speech of Jeremiah's enemies, a declaration of innocence, and a request for vengeance. They're found in chapters 11, 12, 15, 17, 18, and 20.

The one in chapter 20 reveals Jeremiah is mad at God. He feels used, at first complaining about jeers from others. However, the mood later changes, and Jeremiah moves from despair to determination.

The Second Theme

In 597 BCE, Jerusalem was conquered, and 10,000 captives were taken to Babylon. The last king of Judah, Zedekiah, ruled from 596 to 586. Almost immediately, he rebelled against Babylon, who were soon at the gates.

Jeremiah's advice, recorded in chapter 21, is to surrender. That's treason; Jeremiah appears to be giving solace to the enemy. There is an attempt on Jeremiah's life in chapter 38 by the court officials, even though Zedekiah continues to meet with Jeremiah.

During the long siege of 587, there is an emphasis on hope, tying in with the second theme of building and planting. Part of this hope is theological. Chapters 30–32 contain the largest concentration of the phrase "You will be my people and I will be your God" anywhere in the Old Testament. This is what scholars call the covenant formula.

UNDERSTANDING THE OLD TESTAMENT

This new covenant should not be thought of in the Christian sense that Paul writes about in the New Testament. The issue is not that the old covenant was about a law, and the new covenant lacks law. The distinction is the location of the law. In other words, it is not an external law to obey but an internal law—a moral compass.

Jeremiah

LECTURE 17 | JEREMIAH, PERSECUTED PROPHET

Jeremiah had already said in 17:1 that the people had sin written on their hearts, so this promise is that God will erase it and give them the ability to follow the law by his own action. The outcome of this is that they will know God, as many of the prophets said was essential for practicing justice. The reason they will know God, according to verse 34, is because he will forgive their sins.

The next chapter says that the hope is also material. During a lull in fighting, God commands Jeremiah to buy land in Anatoth, his ancestral home behind enemy lines. There's no way to get there. It's overrun by the Babylonians. But God tells Jeremiah to make the purchase, because "Houses, fields and vineyards shall again be purchased in this land." There will be a return from this exile.

God is signaling that although the Jews may go into exile now, facing seemingly overwhelming obstacles to going home, one day they will be able to return. In effect, God pledges that he intends to rebuild—and replant.

Questions to Consider

- ✡ Does it matter if the confessions of Jeremiah are a literary invention rather than the words or thoughts of Jeremiah?
- ✡ Is it legitimate to accuse Jeremiah of treason and sedition?

Suggested Reading

Brueggemann, *To Pluck Up, to Tear Down*.

——, *To Build, to Plant*.

DANIEL AND APOCALYPTIC LITERATURE

LECTURE 18

The book of Daniel was assembled very late in the compilation of the Old Testament. It introduces a different genre—apocalyptic literature—that isn't prevalent elsewhere in the Old Testament. Apocalyptic literature derives from prophetic literature. It involves revelation initiated by God, delivered through a mediator such as an angel to a holy person. In general, it has to do with the end of time.

Dating the Book

Much of it is written in Aramaic, not Hebrew. There are also many loaned words from Persian and even Greek in the book. The Jews were not exposed to the Persian language until around the year 500 BCE and not to Greek until around the year 300 BCE. Additionally, much of the book seems directly related to the persecution of Jews in the 2nd century BCE.

LECTURE 18 | DANIEL AND APOCALYPTIC LITERATURE

Some of the book is older than that, perhaps going back to the 6th century BCE. Much of the book originated as late as 150 BCE. The book of Daniel is a collection of prophetic oracles and stories, some of them familiar, like Daniel in the lion's den. The oldest parts of Daniel are chapters 4 and 5.

Elements of Apocalyptic Literature

The latest chapters of Daniel have to be 8 through 12. These seem directly tied to the persecution of the Jewish people in the 2nd century BCE by the Syrian Greek ruler, Antiochus Epiphanes.

Daniel in the lions den

The book of Daniel includes alternating sections of narratives and apocalypses. While many apocalypses do envision the end of time—and salvation at the end of time—they are about disclosing a transcendent reality. For example, take Daniel 8:16:

> I heard a human voice that cried out, "Gabriel explain the vision to this man." When he came near where I was standing, I fell prostrate in terror. But he said to me, "Understand, O Son of Man, the vision refers to the end time."

This mediation by an angelic being, in this case Gabriel. It is in the book of Daniel that angels are first given names. The content is explicitly about the end of time.

Another element of biblical apocalyptic literature is dualism, meaning the presentation of contrary pairs. Examples include this age versus the age to come, the evil many versus the righteous few, and heaven mirroring earth. These are conflicts between people on earth understood as reflecting struggles between supernatural powers.

The apocalyptic worldview is if you are persecuted, it might be because you are righteous and other people in power are the sinners. Justice is postponed until God interrupts history. God will eventually reward good with good and evil with evil—but not right now.

Another important element of apocalyptic literature is symbolic numbers, animals, and code words. For example, the vision that Daniel 8 refers to is described in the preceding verses, painting a picture of aggressive horned beasts. They symbolized different nations and peoples.

Innovations

The book of Daniel brings along with it a number of theological innovations. One of these is a major contribution to Judaism's developing messianism, the elaboration of the notion of a messiah, or promised redeemer.

We see this in Daniel chapter 7. One interpretation of this chapter comes from the work of the great Jewish scholar Daniel Boyarin, in his book *The Jewish Gospels*. There are two figures in this section. The first is the Ancient of Days, which is clearly God.

LECTURE 18 | DANIEL AND APOCALYPTIC LITERATURE

The second is the Son of Man. The scholar Daniel Boyarin says this means either a deified human or God incarnate. The Son of Man is given power over earth, is enthroned in heaven, is younger than God, is human-like, and is also divine. These characteristics belonging to the Messiah form a central tenet of Christianity, the divinity of Jesus.

Confirmation that the title Son of Man already had these notions before the time of Jesus comes from a book of the Apocrypha called 1 Enoch. This is a huge book that was immensely popular. Many copies are found in the Dead Sea Scrolls.

Stores in Daniel

Interspersed with the apocalyptic material are six stories in Daniel, in chapters 1, 3, 4, 6, 13, and 14. In each of these, there is a Jewish wise man who is an interpreter of dreams and mysterious writing. In another sense, the stories feature faithful Jews whom God saves.

Chapter 1 presents the narrative context in which all of these stories are set. Verse 1 depicts the fall of Jerusalem, which was accompanied by the exile of many people, among whom are Daniel and his friends, Hannaiah, Mishael, and Azariah.

Fall of Jerusalem

Verse 2 is explicit that the Lord handed all of Judah over to Nebuchadnezzar. Later on, the royal servant Ashpenaz refers to Nebuchadnezzar as his "lord." This story will be about which lord Daniel and his friends will serve.

The Jews were not only militarily overwhelmed. They were surely culturally overwhelmed. They had gone from a cultural backwater of the hills of Judah to a society that had known literature for millennia as well as scientific, medicinal, and geographic knowledge.

The narrative presents the Babylonian king setting about to remove the young men's native culture so as to make wise men out of them. In verse 5, it is relayed that "The King allotted them a daily portion of food and wine from the royal table. After three years training, they were to enter the king service." Then, "The Chief Chamberlain changed their names: Daniel to Belteshezzar, Hannaiah to Shadrach, Mishael to Meshach, and Azariah to Abednego."

Verse 7 states that the chief chamberlain "determined" their names. That's not the normal phrase for naming people, but it's exactly the word used in the next verse: "Daniel *determined* not to defile himself with the king's food." This contrasts two worldviews: that of the Babylonians and that of the Israelites.

It's not clear what the problem with the food is. It doesn't seem to be about kosher food. It is likely that the issue is one of identity: Food is tied up with ethnicity, and part of the way to indoctrinate someone in a new culture is to force them to change their diet.

Daniel proposes a test. In verse 12, he says, "Test your servants for ten days. Let us be given vegetables to eat and water to drink. Then see how we look in comparison with the young men who eat from the royal table." We discover the result of this in verse 15: "After ten days, they looked healthier and better fed than any of the young men who ate from the royal table." The young men go on to be the king's chief advisers.

This is a message for diaspora Jews, living under foreign domination. And the message is the same as found in the apocalyptic sections: No matter what, do not give up your faith. God will deliver you.

LECTURE 18 | DANIEL AND APOCALYPTIC LITERATURE

Questions to Consider

- ✡ If apocalyptic literature gave hope to persecuted people, what was its message to people in times of prosperity?

- ✡ What do the stories of Daniel say to persecuted people? What do they say to Jews in times of prosperity?

Suggested Reading

Boyarin, *The Jewish Gospels*.

Collins, "From Prophecy to Apocalypticism."

QUIZ 3

1. Upon Elijah's victory over the prophets of Baal, he:
a. kills Ahab and Jezebel
b. prays for death
c. rebuilds a temple to Yahweh
d. flees to a widow's home

2. Ahasuerus invited everyone, even the commoners, to his banquet so that they:
a. could admire the spectacle
b. would give him popular support
c. could defend Mordechai
d. could attack the Jews

3. Which of the following does Amos not accuse Israel's leaders of?
a. drinking wine from bowls
b. inventing musical instruments
c. riding the choicest camels
d. sprawling on couches while dining

4. Isaiah says the Messiah will sprout from the:
a. root of Ruth
b. stump of Jesse
c. seed of Solomon
d. soil of Saul

QUIZ 3

5. Jeremiah accuses the king of painting his palace:

a. scarlet red
b. Chartreuse green
c. royal blue
d. fuchsia

6. Daniel proves he can be permitted to dine according to Jewish law by asking that he and his friends be fed only:

a. bacon
b. matzo crackers
c. falafel
d. vegetables

Answers: 1.(b); 2.(a); 3.(c); 4.(b); 5.(a); 6.(d)

HOW SCHOLARS STUDY PSALMS

LECTURE 19

This lecture looks at the book of Psalms and examines the lyrics of the psalms—or songs—contained within. The psalms are prayers in addition to being songs. Whereas much of the Bible reads as the word of God directed to humans, psalms read as the words of humans to God.

Parallelism

The psalms are Hebrew poetry, which is marked by parallelism. Parallelism means the correspondence of lines, usually in pairs. This can be correspondence of syntax, morphology, or meaning. Most of the terminology used to describe parallelism from the Anglican bishop Robert Lowth, who lived in the 1700s.

Parallelism works in one of two ways. In synonymous parallelism, the same thought is echoed. For example, in Psalm 113:7, take this echoed thought: "He raises the poor from the dust and lifts the needy from the ash heap."

On the other hand, one can express an opposing thought in the second line. This is called antithetic parallelism. Consider Psalm 126:5: "Those who sow in tears shall reap with shouts of joy." It's metaphorical. Metaphor is a major part of what makes the psalms poetry. This isn't about literal sowing and reaping. It's about planning and enjoying the results.

The psalm authors are very skilled at using parallelism to map out large patterns in a psalm. For instance, the first verse may not correspond to the second. Imagine that the first verse corresponds to the last verse, and the second verse corresponds to the penultimate verse. This is called a chiasm.

In Psalm 22, verses 1 and 11, there are words that correspond to each other in some way. Both verses are pleas to God to not abandon the one praying. Verses 1 and 11 are in parallelism with each other. That means that the entire unit of verses 1 through 11 is designated by inclusion. There are other examples of inclusion throughout the book of Psalms.

A Difficult Passage

Understanding parallelism can also help with difficult passages. For instance, the final stanza of Psalm 137 is addressed to Babylon. It is in the context of the exile of Jews in Babylon after the Babylonians conquered Jerusalem in 586 BCE: "Blessed shall be he who takes your little children and dashes them against the rocks."

At first, it seems Israel is calling for the massacre of innocent children. However, the true reading lies in parallelism. The prior verse is this: "Blessed shall be he who repays you what you have done to us."

The phrase "your little children and dashes them against the rocks" stands in poetic parallelism with "repays you what you have unto us." This isn't about Babylonian babies and all. It's about Israelite babies. It is about coming to terms with what happened in the conquest of Jerusalem in 586. This is a way Israel can say, "You massacred our infants," without saying it directly. The point is not a wish against Babylon; the point is articulating the pain.

Names of the Psalms

It is possible that the verse numbers used in this lecture do not match those in your Bible. The reason for this is the titles, but not the titles that modern editors have added, like "A Prayer for Thanksgiving."

There are actual titles on 116 of the psalms that have been passed down in the manuscripts of the Hebrew text. This affects verse numbering because almost none of the modern English translations of the psalms give those titles a verse number. The Hebrew Bibles give the title verse number 1, and so do the Jewish translations and the New American Bible, which is a Catholic translation. The other translations do not number the titles.

The 116 titles are mostly in psalms 1 through 89. Some of these are musical notation of one type or another. Sometimes, they indicate the type of composition or what the tune is. Sometimes, we are told what the tune is. Some of the titles give instrumentation.

Seventy-three of the psalms are designated "le-David." That could mean "by David," or "for David," or "dedicated to David." Some of them are clearly intended to mean "by David." These tell of an event in David's life when he supposedly composed the psalm.

It's because of this that people often speak of the psalms being written by King David, the shepherd boy who became Israel's second king. However, some of the psalms are attributed to other individuals, including Moses and Solomon.

LECTURE 19 | HOW SCHOLARS STUDY PSALMS

However, some problems set in. A number of times, the contents of a psalm that is le-David speaks of things that didn't exist in David's time, especially the Temple of Jerusalem, which wasn't built until David's son Solomon. Additionally, sometimes the historical note in the title clashes with the account of the episode described in the historical books of the Old Testament.

Solomon Dedicates the Temple of Jerusalem

For instance, the title of Psalm 90 is completely at odds with 2 Samuel 8:13 and 1 Chronicles 18:12. The psalm title says Joab defeated 12,000 men. The historical books have 18,000. Here, the victorious general is named Joab; in Samuel, it's David himself. In the account in the book of Chronicles, it's someone named Abishai. But it's never Joab.

Scholars have suspected for a long time that the titles were apparently added later to the psalms. A 5th-century CE Christian writer from Syria named Theodoret of Cyr surmised that someone added a title without an understanding of the psalm's history or meaning. Titles don't necessarily belong with the psalms in the original, and that's why many Bibles don't give them verse numbers.

The titles do, however, group the psalms into clusters. There are four Davidic collections. There are also psalms of the Sons of Korah. Korah was Aaron the high priest's cousin, who got swallowed up by the earth in desert wanderings with Moses on account of his complaining.

Five Books

As early as the 3rd century CE, people spoke about the psalms being five books. Since 1881, English Bibles—although not all of them—have been marking these five sections or five so-called books out.

The key is that there are nearly repeated doxologies at four places in the book of Psalms, and these doxologies don't look like they belong to the psalms themselves. For instance, take a look at this from 41:13: "Blessed is the Lord, God of Israel, from eternity to eternity. Amen and Amen." Nearly the same wording appears again at 72:18–19, at 89:52, and at 106:48, which repeats Psalm 41 verbatim but adds words from Deuteronomy 27:16–17.

Those doxologies mark out five sections. Then, Psalm 150 in its entirety serves as the doxology. Book 1, or psalms 1–41, ends at exactly the point where the first Davidic collection of psalms ends. Book 2, or 42–72, runs from the start of the Korah psalms to the end of the second Davidic set. Book 3, or 73–89, ends where the concentration of titles overall ends. Book 4 takes place from 90–106. Book 5 covers 107–150.

LECTURE 19 | HOW SCHOLARS STUDY PSALMS

Questions to Consider

- ✡ How might we go about reconstructing performance settings that may have gone with the Psalms originally?
- ✡ Should the Psalms titles be given verse numbers or not? Why?

Suggested Reading

Miller, *The Psalms as Israel's Prayer and Our Own.*

Wendland, *Analyzing the Psalms.*

THE MUSIC OF THE PSALMS
LECTURE 20

This lecture explores the main way in which biblical scholars study the book of Psalms. Doing so is helpful for understanding what's actually at work in the individual psalms.

Three Questions

When biblical scholars approach a psalm, they ask three questions: Who is speaking? Who is addressed? What is the intent? Scholars are still working on these questions in the wake of the early 20th-century German biblical scholar Herman Gunkel, who has influenced the study of psalms more than any other figure.

To the first question—regarding who is speaking—Gunkel proposed three options. First, the speaker could be an individual. Second, the speaker could be a group; in that case, the psalm is called communal or collective.

LECTURE 20 | THE MUSIC OF THE PSALMS

Gunkel's third category was called royal psalms. He only found 10 of these, and most scholars have thrown out the category altogether.

As for the second question—regarding who is speaking—most of the psalms are addressed to God. Some are addressed to someone else. For the third question—regarding the intent—Gunkel's three areas were hymns, thanksgivings, and laments. Hymns and thanksgivings are positive expressions. A lament is a complaint that asks for God's assistance.

Hymns praise God in general terms for his greatness, for his faithfulness as creator and ruler of history. Thanksgivings, on the other hand, thank God for precise gifts—that is, for precise acts of beneficence.

Communal laments typically complain about war, famine, plague, and drought. Individual laments tend to complain about issues like sickness and false accusation.

The Transfer of the Ark of the Covenant by the Singing and Dancing David. Pieter van Lint. c. 1650.

Speculative Genres

At times, scholars have been a little more adventurous or speculative in suggesting genres. There are psalms that quite possibly have been pilgrimage songs. For example, take Psalm 122: "I rejoiced when they said to me 'Let us go to the house of the Lord.' And now our feet are standing within your gates, O Jerusalem." It's addressed from one person to another. Scholars have tentatively suggested that this is a song sung by pilgrims visiting Jerusalem, processing into the city.

Other psalms suggest some sort of ritual or liturgy. Psalm 95 has lines like, "Enter. Let us bow down in worship; let us kneel before the Lord." So do Psalms 15 and 24. Additionally, some of these so-called minor genres are addressed to God.

Distinct Formats

The second half of Gunkel's intellectual enterprise is fascinating. Having divided the psalms into discrete genres—such as individual laments or communal thanksgivings—Gunkel discovered that these genres happen to have distinct formats.

The thanksgiving has a very simple form. It consists of four parts. First, there is a statement declaring thanks for God's acts or attributes. Second is a description of past distress. Third is a testimony where the psalmist tells how God helped them. Finally, there is a declaration of thanks or a promise to praise.

An example is Psalm 18, a long thanksgiving. First is the declaration of thanks: "I love you, Lord." Then, there comes a description of past distress: "Cords of death encompassed me; torrents of destruction terrified me."

Then, the third element is the testimony: "In my distress, I called out: 'Lord!' I cried out to my God. From his temple he heard my voice; my cry to him reached his ears." God comes to the rescue. Eventually, matters end with another praise: "The Lord lives! Blessed be my rock!"

Hymns have a very simple format. Hymns consist of a call to praise, then the motive with the Hebrew word *ki* (meaning "because"), and then a repeat of the call to praise.

LECTURE 20 | THE MUSIC OF THE PSALMS

A lament also has a format, though it's more complex. There are seven parts. In a long psalm, parts might repeat. In a short psalm, a part might be left out. The parts are:

1. A general cry to God.
2. A stated problem.
3. A request or petition for help.
4. An avowal of innocence.
5. A profession of trust.
6. A promise to thank God.
7. Actual praise.

The Purpose

There is a reason for this format. The psalms are doing something psychologically. The Old Testament scholar Walter Brueggemann has said, "There is a close correspondence between the anatomy of the lament psalm and the anatomy of the soul."

In the lament format, the Israelite is praying a lament psalm. The lament actively embraces angst, grief, and anger, and then it moves on to trust and thanksgiving. It's ancient Israelite therapy, so to speak. There are also ancient Near Eastern incantations that begin with an address of praise to a god using his standardized titles. These move to a petition, and finally move to a promise to praise and attract new devotees to that god.

The psalms reflect raw emotions. The writers of the psalms were convinced that God wanted to hear all of those emotions.

Suggested Reading

Brueggemann, *Spirituality of the Psalms*.

PROVERBS IN THE BIBLE: WISDOM LITERATURE
LECTURE 21

This lecture is an introduction to the Old Testament genre of wisdom literature and to the book of Proverbs specifically. Imagery from Proverbs became repeatedly re-used in later religious traditions in fascinating ways.

Hokhma

Scholars translate a specific Hebrew term, *Hokhma*, as meaning "wisdom." However, *Hokhma* has a fairly wide meaning. It can mean the kind of knowledge of cultural traditions that is found especially in non-literature cultures. This knowledge of cultural traditions includes etiquette, rules of jurisprudence, and practical skill.

LECTURE 21 | PROVERBS IN THE BIBLE: WISDOM LITERATURE

The word *Hokhma* is applied in the Bible to the abilities of many different kinds of people. For instance, in Exodus 35:31–35, carpenters have *Hokhma*. In Exodus 28:3, tailors who make the priestly vestments have *Hokhma*.

That definition of *Hokhma* helps explain why much of the wisdom literature in the book of Proverbs and elsewhere seems to be borrowed from literature of other peoples and lightly adapted to Israel. Biblical writers recognized the value of wisdom from Mesopotamia, Egypt, Arabia, and eventually from Greece.

Instructions and Attribution

There are several forms in which wisdom literature appears in the Old Testament. In the book of Proverbs, there are instructions. The literary image is of a wise figure passing wisdom to his son or disciple. 1 Kings 4:32 says that Solomon composed such proverbs.

The classic study of the nature of proverbs in general as a literary form is Archer Taylor's 1931 masterpiece *The Proverb*. He makes a point that is very valid for the book of Proverbs. For example, Proverbs 1:1 says, "Proverbs of Solomon son of David, king of Israel." As Taylor writes, such sayings are timeless, and he says we have to be careful to whom we attribute them.

Most of the books of wisdom literature in the Old Testament are ascribed to Solomon or associated with Solomon. Most likely, they were not by Solomon: In ancient Israel, Solomon's name meant "wisdom." Just as Israelites associated laws with Moses and music with King David, they thought of Solomon as the father genius of this genre.

The actual collection of sayings in the book of Proverbs is generally thought to be from around the 6th century BCE and later. It reflects a wealthy agricultural and urban community. However, these sayings had circulated for centuries by oral tradition.

The book of Proverbs can be divided into nine sections, each with its own superscription, or supposed collector. For example, chapters 1 through 9 are ascribed to Solomon, son of David, king of Israel. The section from chapter 10 through chapter 22:16 is composed of a collection of randomly arranged proverbs about everyday occurrences, attributed to Solomon.

Much of the book of Proverbs was borrowed from foreign traditions. For example, there are several Egyptian elements in Proverbs. The verse 22:2 says, "The Lord weighs the heart." The weighing of a heart is an Egyptian image. Additionally, one line of thinking argues that biblical authors actually borrowed the idea of wisdom as a woman from the Egyptian Maat.

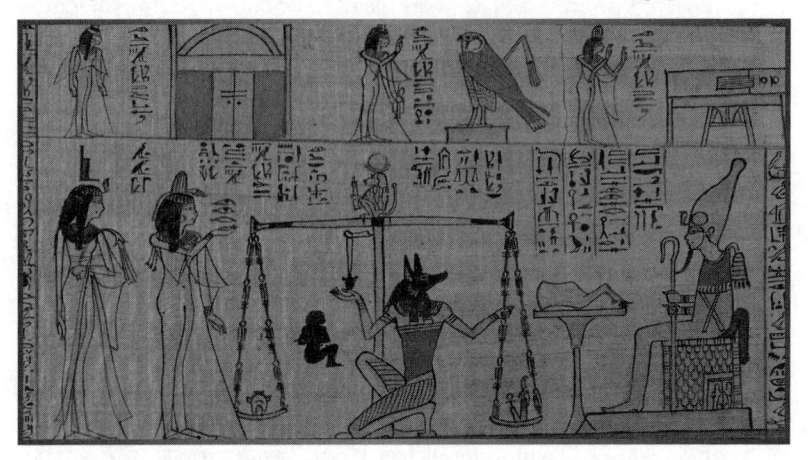

Part of this personification is simply based on the fact that *Hokhma* is a feminine noun. However, there is still a possibility that this personification is being borrowed from Egypt, given that they are borrowing from *Amenemope* and the weighing of the heart.

The First Collection

The first collection in Proverbs features a structure based on pairs of metaphors: two ways, two companions, and two hearts. The two ways are not literal paths, but they build on a metaphor of life as a journey. One path has to do with equity and a good course. The other has to do with evil.

At the end of chapter 2, the second metaphor kicks in. Verse 16 relates that wisdom "will save you from the strange woman." The word translated as "strange" is *Zarah*. This is the counterpart to Lady Wisdom, who is wisdom personified. Just as there are two ways through life, there are two companions.

LECTURE 21 | PROVERBS IN THE BIBLE: WISDOM LITERATURE

Chapter three moves a third metaphor: two hearts. Verse 1 provides the instruction: "My son, do not forget my teaching, but let your heart retain my commandments; for they will bestow on you length of days, years of life and well-being." The opposite part of the "malicious heart" finally appears in chapter 6, verses 12 through 15. The text keeps playing with these three pairs of metaphors all the way through the first nine chapters.

The first unit of the book is a finely crafted literary piece using three pairs of metaphors. It prepares the reader to understand the contents of the whole book.

The reader is prepared to think of the wise sayings as guides for two roads: The reader wants to be on one, not the other. The reader should want one woman and not the other as a companion. The sayings need to be impressed on the reader's heart. Then, the rest of the book of Proverbs actually provides the content.

Questions to Consider

✡ Does Proverbs have a simplistic view of life: Follow this advice, and everything will work out fine?

✡ Why did biblical authors borrow more from their neighbors in wisdom literature than elsewhere?

Suggested Reading

Murphy, *The Tree of Life*.

Taylor, *The Proverb*.

JOB'S SUFFERING AND UNDERSTANDING
LECTURE 22

This lecture focuses on the book of Job. It follows the book's storyline through its climax. At that point, the lecture explores several possibilities about what the text means.

The Beginning of the Text

Chapter 1 features a character called the Satan, which is not the same Satan as in later Jewish and Christian theology. The term *Satan* here is a noun that means "accuser." God praises his servant Job as "blameless and upright, fearing God and avoiding evil." However, the Satan replies that Job does so because God is rewarding him.

LECTURE 22 | JOB'S SUFFERING AND UNDERSTANDING

The satan's argument is that sincere love for God is a lie. Religion is a camouflage for motivations that are economic, social, political, psychological, and cultural. God is ready to take him up on this challenge. In verse 12, "The Lord said to the Satan, 'Very well. All that he has is in your power. Only do not lay a hand on him.'"

In the rest of the prologue, all of Job's children are killed. Job loses all of his property. However, Job is still righteous. The Satan asks for permission to strike him a little closer to home, and Job is hit with great illness. Job's wife says, "Curse God and die." Job refuses and says that he will not reject God.

The Dialogue

Eventually, three friends appear to "comfort" Job. Chapters 4 through 31 are a poetic dialogue between Job and his three friends. The three friends—Eliphaz, Bildad, and Zophar—argue that good things happen to good people, and bad things happen to bad people, and so Job must have done something wrong.

Job suffering

The argument of Eliphaz accuses Job of undermining religion. In Job 15:4, Eliphaz says, "You, in fact, do away with piety, you lessen devotion towards God." In other words, if people believe that Job has done no wrong and suffers anyway, then they're not going to worship God. They're going to think there's no reward for being good, and they won't be good.

Job fundamentally agrees with the theology of his friends. He is upset, because he knows he has done no wrong and he is suffering. Job wants a chance to argue his innocence to God directly.

God's Appearance

In chapter 38, God appears out of the whirlwind, exactly as Job has asked for. God proceeds over the next several chapters to ask questions that Job cannot possibly answer (but God can).

Eventually, though, the book shifts back into prose. God restores Job's prosperity, gives him a new set of children, and makes him very rich and prosperous. Job lives to be 140 years old and see his great-grandchildren.

Job with his children

LECTURE 22 | JOB'S SUFFERING AND UNDERSTANDING

Different Interpretations

Throughout the centuries, readers have been left wondering what just happened and what the book is saying. In verse 5 of chapter 42, the fact that Job says, "I had heard of you by the hearing of the ear, but now my eye has seen you" has led interpreters over the centuries to think God's appearance alone is the answer.

The early Christian writer Augustine thought this was what the book argued, as did the 20th-century Jewish philosopher Martin Buber. Job asked for personal contact with God, and he received it.

A second explanation of God's answer is that Job is simply browbeaten into submission. However, Job never doubted God's power. Instead, he repeatedly spoke of it in chapters 9 and 12, for example.

A third explanation builds on the mention of Job in the New Testament book of James. James 5:11 states, "Indeed we call blessed those who have persevered. You have heard of the perseverance of Job, and you have seen the purpose of the Lord, because the Lord is compassionate and merciful."

If this verse presents Job as the model of perseverance, then perhaps the book is a how-to manual for suffering: One should follow the example of Job, who suffers without losing his faith. It doesn't quite work, however, because it's quite clear that Job is chastised by God and has something to repent about.

A fourth understanding of the book has appeared in some fictional retellings. Archibald McLeish's famous play *J. B.* is basically the book of Job set in the 20th century. Robert Frost wrote *The Mask of Job*. Both interpret the story as ironic and cynical. According to this view, God is a bully, and Job is rightly bitter at the arbitrary way he's been treated.

However, this explanation ascribes to the ancient Israelite authors a philosophy that is hard to imagine them having. Additionally, it is hard imagine centuries of Judaism passing this book down if its message was that God is a blowhard.

God's Two Points

Another interpretation is based on God's two points. God's first point is that Job doesn't understand the intricate workings of the world. Job also doesn't comprehend the nature of God, because that's impossible.

God's second point is this: God is upholding the world according to his plan; however, justice isn't always retributive. For instance, in chapter 39, God asks if Job knows anything about ostriches. He proceeds to describe the ostrich as the most ridiculous creature imaginable. It forgets where its eggs are, and it steps on them and crushes them.

The point is that the natural world is filled with examples where things don't appear just. God says it is all under his control. God denies retributive justice, although he can be retributive, and he is at the end of the book when he restores Job's fortunes.

Job Restored to Prosperity, Laurent de La Hyre (1648)

LECTURE 22 | JOB'S SUFFERING AND UNDERSTANDING

The principles of the order of the universe are not superficial, and order cannot be assumed in a superficial way. Job repents, then, not of sins—not of cockiness—but of the same viewpoint that his friends had.

This explanation of the book of Job really only explains the lesson Job learns: You can't fully understand God. God has things under control, but his justice isn't always retributive.

However, the prologue presumes justice usually is retributive. The satan points out Job is good, and God rewards him. The prologue assumes retributive justice is God's default mode. An explanation of the book has to take into account the prologue.

That raises the question: Why did God take the bet? The answer is that Job matters. The satan is impugning Job's reputation. Job thinks God doesn't care about him. However, not only does God care about him, but this entire episode has taken place because God is defending Job's reputation. By this reading, humans are so important that God will suspend his justice for their reputation.

Questions to Consider

- ✡ Does God treat Job maliciously in the book of Job?
- ✡ How is the Satan in Job different from Satan in later Jewish and Christian tradition?

Suggested Reading

Breakstone, MacLeish, Frost, and Singer, *Job*.

Tsevat, *The Meaning of the Book of Job and Other Biblical Studies*.

ECCLESIASTES AND THE "VANITY OF VANITIES"
LECTURE 23

This lecture focuses on the book of Ecclesiastes. Many people who study this book find little hope in it. However, the book actually has a very profound message to it, which is revealed after the book's meaning is unpacked.

Situating the Book

Most Bibles refer to this book as Ecclesiastes, but some Bibles call the book Qohelet. The Hebrew term *Qohelet* can be translated as meaning "someone who picks at ideas." And the first-person author in this book is named Qohelet. The book opens with: "The words of David's son Qohelet, king in Jerusalem." Qohelet seems to be identified with King Solomon, son of Israel's king, David.

LECTURE 23 | ECCLESIASTES AND THE "VANITY OF VANITIES"

Solomon couldn't have written this book. Solomon lived in the 9th century BCE. This is a very late book in the Old Testament collection. It was probably written somewhere between 275 and 250 BCE. That's the Hellenistic period, when Greek rule and Greek culture infiltrated Judea and Jewish society.

This raises a question: Why has the author chosen to put Solomon at the beginning of this book? In ancient Israel, the name Solomon meant "wisdom." He was thought of as an overarching genius.

This book is ascribed to Solomon. The book of Proverbs is ascribed to Solomon. An even later book in the Apocrypha is called Wisdom of Solomon. By putting Solomon into verse 1, the book is telling you the book contains practical advice on how to go through life and live happily.

Perceived Hopelessness

The second verse of the book sets out the argument: "vanity of vanities, says Qohelet; vanity of vanities—all things are vanity." The term *vanity* here doesn't mean obsession over one's looks; instead it's referring to futility—that is, doing something in vain. And "vanity of vanities" would be a superlative meaning "complete, utter futility."

Everything is arbitrary. Death cancels everything out. This idea is present in many places throughout Ecclesiastes. This is why many readers find the book hopeless.

A Repeating Structure

The book has a hidden structure. The pattern begins to emerge in chapter 3, using the phrase "I saw." In verse 16, there is an experience that challenges Qohelet's traditional views: "And still under the sun in the judgment place, I saw wickedness, wickedness also in the seat of justice." He points out something that he has experienced; he saw wickedness in the courtroom, where one would expect there to be justice.

The second element of the repeating structure involves the phrase "I remembered." Verse 17 goes on to say: "I remembered both the just and the wicked God will judge, since the time is set for every affair and for every work." He sees something bad, and traditional wisdom explains how he should understand what he sees.

However, for Qohelet, this isn't the end of matters. The third part of this repeating structure is an antithesis that begins along the lines of, "I reflected." Verse 18 reads, "So I said in my heart, 'As for human beings, it's God's ways of testing them and showing that they are themselves like beasts.'"

Qohelet also thinks about how both humans and animals perish. This raises a question: Is there really judgment when everyone has died, the just and the unjust perish exactly the same, and the same fate awaits them? Maybe there isn't actually justice.

The fourth element of this repeating structure involves Qohelet providing encouragement. Ecclesiastes 3:22 advises, "I saw there's nothing better for mortals than to rejoice in their work, for this is their lot."

The Book's Meaning

To many, the book provides a bleak message. However, there are several factors that push back against such a view. For example, the author never appears irritated, despondent, or unhappy. He can make readers feel that way, but the author doesn't seem to feel that way.

Additionally, the book is full of advice about what to do. For example, in chapter 7, verse 10, the author seems to think that God intends humanity to adopt a better life, to have real wisdom, and to know some general principles. The book is Solomonic. The book is meant to be wisdom, not despair.

Not all of the readers through history have found the book to be overly negative. For example, Ecclesiastes is read on one of the most important holidays in the Jewish calendar. It is read on the Feast of Sukkoth or Booths, which is the most joyous of all Jewish holidays.

LECTURE 23 | ECCLESIASTES AND THE "VANITY OF VANITIES"

The fourth element in the repeating structure tells the reader to go out and enjoy life. For example, take this line from chapter 3: "I know there is nothing better … than to rejoice and do well during life. Moreover that all can eat and drink and enjoy the good of all their toil this is a gift of God."

The power to enjoy life is itself a divine gift, and the book mocks those who furtively grasp for pleasure on their own. Life is a gift from God, and one has to accept it as a gift with joy rather than anxiety. And failure to enjoy life's blessings is a sin.

Questions to Consider

- Is the epilogue of Qohelet consistent with the rest of the book?
- Where do you come down on Qohelet: Is it optimistic or pessimistic?

Suggested Reading

Lohfink, *Qoheleth*.

SLAYING THE DRAGONS OF THE OLD TESTAMENT

LECTURE 24

This lecture goes back through the entirety of the Old Testament through one lens in particular. Woven through the entire text is a metaphor that is a glimpse of a story of dragon slaying. It's a very important metaphor, because understanding where it comes from—and where it leads—summarizes the message of the corpus as a whole.

Dragons in the Bible

The Bible does include mentions of dragons. For example, take Isaiah 27:1, which reads, "On that day, the Lord with his hard and great and strong sword will punish Leviathan the fleeing serpent, Leviathan the twisting serpent; he will slay the dragon that is in the sea."

LECTURE 24 | SLAYING THE DRAGONS OF THE OLD TESTAMENT

Destruction of the Leviathan

The text is personifying evil because the ancient Israelites had a clear sense of the reality of evil. The biblical writers took this image from a narrative story known to their neighbors, the Canaanites, who preceded the Israelites in the Promised Land and continued to be their closest neighbors throughout the early history.

The most important story here is the myth of the god Baal. The Canaanites' religion had a pantheon of gods on the model of a family. There is the high god, El, along with his wife and children: Yamm, Anat, and Baal.

El has decided to retire and leave the governance of the world to a younger deity. At the beginning of our story, he decides to make the god Yamm king, whose name means "the sea." Yamm is also a dragon, meaning he won't be a very good king of the universe.

The other gods tremble in fear, except for the storm god Baal. Baal is also the god of fertility. Baal battles Yamm, and though Baal's initial attack is futile, Baal eventually wins. Later in the text, Baal is praised for his victory in a passage that gives Yamm yet another name: Leviathan.

Baal is now made king and is eventually given a palace on Mount Zaphon, which sits on the Syrian-Turkish border. He has a feast for all the gods, but he foolishly invites death, or Mot, to his feast. Mot dines on Baal and swallows him. This situation is only rectified when Baal's sister, the goddess Anat, cuts him out of Mot.

For the Canaanites of the time, this myth was not about killing reptiles, but rather about where one finds hope against chaos and calamity. Baal stands for order and security. And because the human king of Ugarit was the chief priest of Baal, the king stands for order and stability in the face of life's chaos.

This myth is far, far older than the Canaanites. They seem to have borrowed much of it from peoples who came before them in the ancient Near East. In fact, the myth goes back to the 5th millennium BCE. However, in all of its iterations, the major elements are the same.

The Myth and the Book of Isaiah

The Old Testament uses this myth over and over again to construct metaphors that say something about God. Many examples are found in the book of Isaiah.

LECTURE 24 | SLAYING THE DRAGONS OF THE OLD TESTAMENT

For instance, Isaiah 27:1 contains a quote from the Ugaritic Baal myth: "On that day, the Lord with his hard and great and strong sword will punish Leviathan the fleeing serpent, Leviathan the twisting serpent; he will slay the dragon that is in the sea." The middle section—"Leviathan the fleeing serpent, Leviathan the twisting serpent"—is word-for-word from Ugarit, even though the Ugaritic text is 500 years or so older.

The Isaiah passage is in the future tense. These are eschatological passages—that is, passages about the end of time, predicting the day on which God will make everything right.

The Myth and the Psalms

Elements derived from this myth are also found all over the psalms of the Old Testament. For instance, Psalm 48 refers to Mount Zion, or Jerusalem, as Zaphon.

Psalm 77 features a victory that is set in the past. Verse 16 reads:

> When the waters saw you, O God, when the waters saw you, they were afraid; indeed the deep trembled. The clouds poured out water; the skies gave forth thunder; your arrows flashed on every side. The crash of your thunder was in the whirlwind; your lightings lighted up the world.

In this case, it is Israel's god who is the storm god, not Baal. Then, in verse 19 this information is recounted:

> Your way was through the sea, your path through the great waters; yet your footprints were unseen. You led your people like a flock by the hand of Moses and Aaron.

Now, we're back at the Red Sea, even though in the account in Exodus there's no thunderstorm. This makes it look like God's battle is against the sea itself rather than against the Egyptians. The idea is that each of these moments, like the crossing of the sea, are manifestations of the cosmic power God has to defeat evil.

Psalm 89 in verses 9 and 10 delivers praise for God, who is both creator and dragon slayer:

> You rule the raging of the sea; when its waves rise, you still them. You crushed Rahab like a carcass; you scattered your enemies with your mighty arm. The heavens are yours; the earth also is yours; the world and all that is in it, you have founded them.

A political message follows if you continue reading. The human king stands as the representative of the dragon slayer, as was the case in pre-Israelite myths.

The Myth and the Book of Job

This myth also comes up in the book of Job. This is the story of Job suffering even though he's done nothing wrong. He is trying to figure out why he must suffer. Job and his friends repeatedly refer to the dragon-slaying myth. For instance, at one point, Job asks God, "Am I the sea, or a dragon, that you set a guard over me?"

At the end of the story, something interesting happens. In Job 38:8, God affirms that at creation he defeated the sea. Then, in chapters 40 and 41, he describes Leviathan as "ferocious." He describes Leviathan's armor, teeth, and breathing of fire.

But then, God downplays its ferociousness. That same downgrading of Leviathan occurs in Psalm 104, which speaks of Leviathan as being "made to sport with."

However, overall, there is far more dragon slaying than dragon taming. The reason is that this is deep engagement with human suffering. In the Old Testament, there are two approaches that someone who believed in God could take to understand deep suffering, to answer the question of how an all-powerful, all-good God could permit suffering.

One option is to compromise on the goodness of God—that is, to make him a bit less good to preserve his all-powerful, all-knowing status. The other option is to compromise on God's omnipotence, make him seem a bit less powerful to preserve his all-goodness.

LECTURE 24 | SLAYING THE DRAGONS OF THE OLD TESTAMENT

That means foregoing some traditional ideas of God being in control in favor of the idea that forces of chaos, pictured as a dragon or the sea, sometimes rage. God rages against them. This limits God's power.

That is why the Bible does not always reduce Leviathan. The dragon is defeated by God in far more texts than the dragon is a tame pet. Additionally, the divine warrior is meant to be on the ropes. Initial defeat of the storm god is an integral part of the myth.

Taking the biblical canon as a whole, Genesis 3 is an initial defeat: The serpent won. However, that is not the end of the story. The dragon is always ultimately slain. There is no myth from any culture in which the dragon is unscathed. Ultimately, God is omnipotent.

Questions to Consider

- ✡ Would it matter to Jewish or Christian believers if a basic image of the Old Testament was borrowed from pagan peoples?
- ✡ Did ancient Israelites think there were actual dragons?

Suggested Reading

Angel, *Playing with Dragons*.

Boyd, *God at War*.

Miller, *The Dragon, the Mountain, and the Nations*.

QUIZ 4

1. An example of alliteration would be:
a. Peter Piper picked a peck of pickled peppers.
b. How now brown cow?
c. I start to think, and then I sink—Into the paper like I was ink.
d. He's choking, how? Everybody's joking now.

2. Which of these is not a genre of the Psalms?
a. dialogue
b. curse
c. lament
d. confession

3. Wisdom is personified as a/an:
a. owl
b. grandfather
c. dragon
d. woman

4. Because Job is so difficult to translate and interpret, Jerome likened it to a/an:
a. eel
b. goat
c. dragon
d. banana peel

QUIZ 4

5. Qohelet considers that "everything" in life is:

a. a bowl of cherries
b. a chase after wind
c. breaking wind
d. a box of chocolates

6. The dragon-slaying deity is always depicted as a/an:

a. storm god
b. sun god
c. elderly man
d. hobbit

Answers: 1.(a); 2.(a); 3.(d); 4.(a); 5.(b); 6.(a)

BIBLIOGRAPHY

Angel, Andy. *Playing with Dragons: Living with Suffering and God.* Cambridge: Lutterworth, 2014. Explains how the dragon-slaying metaphor in the Bible is a solution to the problem of how an all-powerful God can allow suffering.

Aubin, Henry. 2003. *The Rescue of Jerusalem: The Alliance between Hebrews and Africans in 701 BC.* Toronto: Anchor Canada. Shows how the approach of an Ethiopian-Egyptian army under an Ethiopian pharaoh forced the Assyrians to abandon their conquest of Judah, thus saving Jerusalem.

Bailey, Wilma Ann. *"You Shall Not Kill" or "You Shall Not Murder"?: The Assault on a Biblical Text.* Collegeville, MN: Liturgical Press, 2005. Explains how 20th-century Bibles changed the wording of the commandment and what it really means in the Ten Commandments.

Bashear, Suliman. "Abraham's Sacrifice of His Son and Related Issues." *Der Islam* 67 (1990): 243–77. Discusses the story of Abraham's offering his son as understood in Islam

Bellis, Alice Ogden. *Helpmates, Harlots, and Heroes: Women's Stories in the Hebrew Bible.* Louisville: Westminster John Knox Press, 2007. The short stories highlight female heroes and "male strengths" that fail because Israel could not appeal to such strengths in the postexilic period. Thus, Ruth, Esther, and Judith stand for Israel.

Bird, Phyllis. "Genesis 1–3 as a Source for a Contemporary Theology of Sexuality." *Ex Auditu* 3 (1987): 31–44. Explores the lack of patriarchy in Genesis 1 and 2, and what brings it about in Genesis 3.

Blenkinsopp, Joseph. *Creation, Un-creation, and Re-creation: A Discursive Commentary on Genesis 1–11.* New York: Continuum, 2011. Explores the ways Genesis 2–3 corresponds to the story of Israel's own history from Exodus to Babylonian Exile.

BIBLIOGRAPHY

Boyarin, Daniel. *The Jewish Gospels: The Story of the Jewish Christ*. New York: The New Press, 2013. Explains the "Son of Man" figure in Daniel, Enoch, and elsewhere as part of developing Jewish concepts of a coming redeemer.

Boyd, Gregory A. *God at War: The Bible & Spiritual Conflict*. Downers Grove: InterVarsity Press, 2014. Explains how the dragon-slaying metaphor in the Bible is a solution to the problem of how an all-powerful God can allow suffering.

Breakstone, Raymond, Archibald MacLeish, Robert Frost, and June Singer. *Job: a Case Study*. New York: Bookman Associates, 1964. Anthology of modern authors who—especially MacLeish and Frost—think God comes off as an arrogant bully.

Brueggemann, Walter. "From Hurt to Joy, from Death to Life." *Interpretation* 28 (1974): 3–19. Examines the psychological impact of the lament Psalms' format.

———. *To Pluck Up, to Tear Down: A Commentary on the Book of Jeremiah 1–25*. Grand Rapids: Eerdmans, 1993. Commentary on Jeremiah focusing on God's determination to punish Israel and Jeremiah's advice to the king to surrender.

———. *To Build, to Plant: A Commentary on Jeremiah 26–52*. Grand Rapids: Eerdmans, 1991. Commentary on Jeremiah focusing on the hope promised, both of return from Exile and of a "new covenant."

———. *Spirituality of the Psalms*. Philadelphia: Augsburg Fortress, 2001. Examines the psychological effect of the format elements of the Psalms.

Campbell, Antony F., and Mark A. O'Brien. *Unfolding the Deuteronomistic History: Origins, Upgrades, Present Text*. Minneapolis: Fortress Press, 2000. Explains what the Deuteronomistic History is, how it came to be, and where its editing is clearest.

Collins, John J. "From Prophecy to Apocalypticism." In *The Encyclopedia of Apocalypticism. 1, 1.*, ed. John J. Collins. New York: Continuum, 2006. Excellent overview of the apocalyptic genre and its appearance in Daniel.

Cook, Stephen L. *Conversations with Scripture: 2 Isaiah*. Harrisburg, PA: Morehouse, 2008. Excellent discussion of the suffering servant and what this figure stands for.

Davis, Ellen "Sabbath: The Culmination of Creation." *Living Pulpit* 7.2 (April 1998): 6–7. Duke University Divinity School scholar explains how the Sabbath is the pinnacle of creation in Genesis 1.

Dhorme, Eduard. *A Commentary on the Book of Job*. Nashville: Nelson, 1984. Classic study showing all of Job was written by the same author, except for the Elihu material.

Eidevall, Göran. *Amos: A New Translation with Introduction and Commentary*. Anchor Bible. New Haven: Yale University Press, 2018. Excellent commentary on Amos that highlights the prophet's condemnation of consumerism.

Finkelstein, Jacob J. *The Ox That Gored*. Philadelphia: American Philosophical Society, 1981. Classic presentation of the parallels of biblical and ancient Near Eastern law.

Fox, Michael V. *Character and Ideology in the Book of Esther*. Eugene, OR: Wipf & Stock, 2010. Highlights the comic portrait of Ahasuerus in Esther and the heroism of Esther.

———. "God's Answer and Job's Response." *Biblica* (2013): 1–23. Moves beyond Tsevat's work to discuss the meaning of Job for the reader.

BIBLIOGRAPHY

Freedman, David Noel. "Divine Commitment and Human Obligation: Covenant Theme." In *Divine Commitment and Human Obligation: Selected Writings of David Noel Freedman*. Ed. John R. Huddlestun. Grand Rapids: Eerdmans, 1997. Classics study explaining the two types of Old Testament covenant, contrasting that with Abraham with that with Moses.

Gordon, Maurice Bear. "Medicine among the Ancient Hebrews," *Isis: The Journal of the History of Science Society* 33 (1941): 454–485. Illustrates how the leprosy procedures in Leviticus constitute scientific inquiry.

Gunkel, Hermann, *The Psalms: A Form-Critical Introduction*. Facet Books Biblical Series 19. Philadelphia: Fortress, 1967. Classic first published in the 1930s providing the basic methods and terminology of Psalms' scholarship.

Habel, Norman C. "The Symbolism of Wisdom in Proverbs 1–9." *Interpretation* 26 (1972): 131–157. Unpacks the "two ways, two hearts, two companions" symbolism of Proverbs 1–9.

Hagedorn, Anselm. "Taking the Pentateuch to the Twenty-First Century." *Expository Times* 119 (2007): 53–58. Updates the scholarship on authorship of the Pentateuch, the decline of the documentary hypothesis, and the state of the field in the early 21st century.

Halpern, Baruch. *David's Secret Demons*. Grand Rapids: Eerdmans, 2004. A book about why you shouldn't like David, discussing the negative portrait of him in the books of Samuel.

Heller, Roy L. *Characters of Elijah and Elisha and the Deuteronomic Evaluation of Prophecy*. London: Bloomsbury, 2018. Details the negative portrait of Elijah in Kings: selfish, vindictive, and complaining.

Heschel, Abraham Joshua. 1969. *The Prophets*. New York: Harper Torchbooks. Classic study of the nature of Hebrew prophecy; still extremely valuable in its insights.

Heskett, Randall. *Messianism within the Scriptural Scroll of Isaiah.* New York: T & T Clark International, 2007. Explains how the last sections of the book of Isaiah are meant to be read alongside sections early in the book.

Ho, Ahuva. *Ṣedeq and Ṣedaqah in the Hebrew Bible.* New York: Peter Lang, 1991. The best study of *tzedekah* righteousness in Amos and the rest of the Old Testament.

Houston, Walter J. *Contending for Justice: Ideologies and Theologies of Social Justice in the Old Testament.* London: T & T Clark, 2008. Discusses the protections of the powerless in the biblical law.

Huddlestun, John R. "Red Sea." In *The Anchor Bible Dictionary.* Ed. David Noel Freedman. Garden City: Doubleday, 1992. Definitive proof that there is no Sea of Reeds and the Exodus story is about the Red Sea.

Johnson, Kathryn A., Andrew E. White, Brenna M. Boyd, and Adam B. Cohen. "Matzah, Meat, Milk, and Mana: Psychological Influences on Religio-Cultural Food Practices." *Journal of Cross-Cultural Psychology* 42 (2011): 1421–1436. Explains how kosher food laws and similar practices promote group identity.

Kaufmann, Yehezkel. *The Babylonian Captivity and Deutero-Isaiah.* New York: Union of American Hebrew Congregations, 1970. Classic study of the meaning of so-called Second and Third Isaiah, especially the treatment of foreigners in the latter.

LaCocque, André *The Trial of Innocence: Adam, Eve, and the Yahwist.* Eugene, OR: Wipf and Stock, 2006. Excellent close reading of Genesis 2–3, unpacking the various meanings intended in the text.

BIBLIOGRAPHY

Levenson, Jon D. "The Exodus and Biblical Theology." *Biblical Theology Bulletin* 26 (1996): 4-10. Points out that God does not deliver Israel in Exodus because he regularly sets captive people free but because of his covenant with Israel, suggesting liberation theology could be cultural appropriation.

Lohfink, Norbert. *Qoheleth: A Continental Commentary.* Minneapolis: Fortress, 2003. Excellent commentary on Qohelet that highlights the joy promoted in the book.

Longman, Tremper. *The Book of Ecclesiastes.* Grand Rapids: Eerdmans, 2007. Another great commentary on Qohelet that emphasizes the joy promoted in the book.

Meyers, Carol *Discovering Eve: Ancient Israelite Women in Context.* New York: Oxford University Press, 1988. Discusses the advent of patriarchy in the words of God to the woman at the end of Genesis 3.

Meynet, Roland. "Two Decalogues, Law of Freedom." *Studia Rhetorica* 16 (2004): 1–35. Explains the use of "serve" in the Ten Commandments and how the commandments guarantee freedom, not slavery.

———. *Called to Freedom.* Miami, Florida: Convivium, 2009. Expansion of the author's 2004 article on the Ten Commandments as a guarantee of freedom.

Middleton, J. Richard. *The Liberating Image: The Imago Dei in Genesis 1.* Grand Rapids: Brazos, 2005. Best analysis of what "made in the image and likeness of God" has meant to interpreters and actually means in the text.

Miller, Robert D., II. *Chieftains of the Highland Clans: A Social History of Israel in the 12th and 11th Centuries BC.* Grand Rapids: Eerdmans, 2005. Repr. Eugene, OR: Wipf & Stock, 2012. Your lecturer explains how to tell Israelites from Canaanites and the relationship of archaeology of the Early Iron Age to the Book of Judges.

———. *The Dragon, the Mountain, and the Nations: An Old Testament Myth, Its Origins, and Its Afterlives*. University Park: Eisenbrauns, 2018. Course lecturer traces the dragon-slaying motif from the Old Testament back to the dawn of time.

———. *The Psalms as Israel's Prayer and Our Own*. New Delhi: Christian World Imprints, 2013. Course lecturer's introduction to the Psalms, surveying poetics, genre, and psychology.

Murphy, Roland E. *The Tree of Life: An Exploration of Biblical Wisdom Literature*. Grand Rapids: Eerdmans, 2002. Introduction to the wisdom genre, explaining what *hokhma* means.

Nayap-Pot, Dalila. "Life in the Midst of Death: Naomi, Ruth, and the Plight of Indigenous Women." In *Vernacular Hermeneutics*. Ed. R. S. Sugirtharajah. Sheffield: Sheffield Academic Press, 1999. Highlights Ruth's predicament and behavior as a foreign migrant in Judah.

Perry, John M. *Exploring the Genesis Creation and Fall Stories*. Kansas City: Sheed and Ward, 1992. Helpful survey of the philosophical points of Genesis 1, especially in how it would be heard by a non-Israelite.

Said, Edward. "Exodus and Liberation: A Canaanite Readin." *Grand Street* 5.2 (Winter, 1986): 86–106. Important 20th-century Palestinian philosopher and activist suggests the Exodus is not theologically valuable for liberation but historically harmful.

Saner, Andrea D. *"Too Much to Grasp": Exodus 3:13–15 and the Reality of God*. Journal of Theological Interpretation Supplement 11. Winona Lake: Eisenbrauns, 2015. Explains what the divine name Yahweh really means, especially as Exodus 3 presents it.

BIBLIOGRAPHY

Seow, Choon Leong. *Daniel.* Westminster Bible Companion. Louisville: Westminster John Knox Press, 2003. Excellent commentary on Daniel that unpacks the stories well, especially the experience of exiles in chapter 1.

Shanks, Hershel, William G. Dever, Baruch Halpern, and P. Kyle McCarter. *The Rise of Ancient Israel: Symposium at the Smithsonian Institution, October 26, 1991, Sponsored by the Resident Associate Program.* Washington DC: Biblical Archaeology Society, 1992. Archaeologists and biblical scholars discuss the Four Models for the advent of Ancient Israel.

Sheriffs, Deryck "Moving on with God: Key motifs in Exodus 13–20." *Themelios* 15.2 (1990): 49–60. South African scholar acknowledges misuse of Exodus in contemporary theology, but suggests positive ways to appropriate the text.

Smith, Mark S. *The Priestly Vision of Genesis 1.* Minneapolis: Fortress, 2009. One of the foremost biblical scholars today unpacks the full meaning of Genesis 1.

Taylor, Archer. *The Proverb.* Hatboro, PA: Folklore Associates, 1962. Classic study of proverbs in every culture of the world.

Tetsutaro, Ariga. "Being and Hāyāh," *Japanese Journal of Religious Studies* 11 (1984): 267–288. Excellent study of the "philosophy" contained in the divine name Yahweh.

Thompson, Thomas L. *The Historicity of the Patriarchal Narratives: The Quest for the Historical Abraham.* Harrisburg, PA: Trinity Press International, 2002. Classic refutation of mid-20th century claims for placing Abraham in the Middle Bronze Age.

Tsevat, Matitiahu. *The Meaning of the Book of Job and Other Biblical Studies: Essays on the Literature and Religion of the Hebrew Bible*. New York: Ktav Publishing House, 1990. Explores various meanings of God's appearance at the end of the book of Job.

Vogels, Walter "The Power Struggle between Man and Woman (Gen. 3:16b)." *Biblica* 77 (1996): 197–209. Discusses the advent of patriarchy in the words of God to the woman at the end of Genesis 3.

Warrior, Robert A. "Canaanites, Cowboys, and Indians," *Christianity and Crisis* 49 (1989): 261–265. American Indian scholar and activist suggests the Exodus is not theologically valuable for liberation but historically harmful.

Webb, Barry G. *The Book of Judges*. Grand Rapids, MI: Eerdmans, 2012. Excellent commentary on Judges that details the downward spiral of the book toward idolatry, injustice, and violence.

Weiss, Herold. *A Day of Gladness: The Sabbath Among Jews and Christians in Antiquity*. Columbia, SC: University of South Carolina Press, 2003. Judaism understands of the Sabbath as a temple in time, a bride to be welcomed, and a foretaste of the world to come.

Wendland, Ernst R. *Analyzing the Psalms*. Dallas: SIL International, 2002. A "workbook" that walks the reader through structural analysis of various Psalms.

Westbrook, Raymond, and Bruce Wells. *Law from the Tigris to the Tiber: The Shared Tradition*. Winona Lake: Eisenbrauns, 2014. Explains how law codes were really school texts in the ancient Near East, while actual laws were oral.

BIBLIOGRAPHY

Whybray, R. Norman. *Introduction to the Pentateuch*. Grand Rapids: Eerdmans, 1995. Especially in first chapters, this book explains how scholars investigate the authorship of the Pentateuch, the conclusions reached in the past, and more recent undermining of those conclusions.

Williamson, H. G. M. *The Book Called Isaiah*. Oxford: Clarendon Press, 2005. Explains how the book of Isaiah was written in phases but ought to be read as a coherent whole.

Wright, David P. "Laws of Hammurabi as a Source for the Covenant Collection (Exodus 20: 23–23: 19)." *Maarav* 10 (2003): 11-87. Shows the parallels between the Covenant Code and the Code of Hammurabi.

Zakovitch, Yair "The Interpretative Significance of the Sequence of Psalms 111–112.113–118.119." In *The Composition of the Book of Psalms*. Ed. Erich Zenger. Leuven: Peeters, 2010. Explains how Psalms can be read consecutively, especially how 111–119 can be read from one to the next and why 114 doesn't belong.

Zenger, Erich. "The Book of Leviticus—An Important Book in Jewish-Christian Dialogue." 40th International Jewish-Christian Bible Week, 2008. Explains why Leviticus is so important for Judaism but not for Christians, and what difference that makes.

IMAGE CREDITS

P#	Credit
4	gldburger/iStock/Getty Images.
6	SAVA COSMIN/Depositphotos.
9	Rijksmuseum, Amsterdam/Public domain.
11	Rijksmuseum, Amsterdam/Public domain.
12	University of Toronto - Robarts Library/Internet Archive/Public domain.
15	Art Institute of Chicago/Public domain.
16	Art Institute of Chicago/Public domain.
20	Anthony/flickr/CC BY-ND 2.0.
22	Rijksmuseum, Amsterdam/Public domain.
26	scaned by:József Molnár/Hungarian National Gallery/Wikimedia commons/Public domain.
29	Caravaggio - scan/Wikimedia commons/Public domain.
32	oceansbridge.com/Wikimedia commons/Public domain.
34	photo by: Usenet/Birmingham Museum and Art Gallery/Wikimedia commons/Public domain.
41	Anonymous (Noord-Nederland)/Wikimedia commons/CC0.
44	Brigham Young University/Internet Archive/Public domain.
47	Philadelphia Museum of Art/Public domain.
50	ZU_09/E+/Getty Images.
53	From Jewish Art, edited by Grace Cohen Grossman/Wikimedia commons/Public domain.
58	Gary Todd/flickr/Public domain.
58	Gary Todd/flickr/Public domain.
60	ZU_09/Getty Images.
63	ZU_09/DigitalVision Vectors/Getty Images.
65	ZU_09/DigitalVision Vectors/Getty Images.
67	The Yorck Project (2002) 10.000 Meisterwerke der Malerei (DVD-ROM), distributed by DIRECTMEDIA/Public domain.
69	Google Art Project/Wikimedia commons/Public domain.
72	ZU_09/DigitalVision Vectors/Getty Images.

IMAGE CREDITS

74	Detroit Institute of Arts, Gift of Mr. and Mrs. John N. Lord/Public domain.
75	Rijksmuseum, Amsterdam/Public domain.
76	The Jewish Museum/Public domain.
83	PHOTOS.com/ Getty Images.
85	sedmak/iStock/Getty Images.
86	British Library/flickr/Public domain.
90	The Jewish Museum/Public domain.
92	National Gallery, London/Wikimedia commons/Public domain.
93	duncan1890/Getty Images.
97	sedmak/iStock/Getty Images.
102	Getty Research Institute/Internet Archive/Public domain.
106	The Providence Lithograph Company/Wikimedia commons/Public domain.
108	ZU_09/DigitalVision Vectors/Getty Images.
111	PHOTOS.com/ Getty Images.
113	National Library of France/Public domain.
120	sedmak/iStock/Getty Images.
121	The Jewish Museum/Public domain.
125	Museum Abtei Liesborn/Wikimedia commons/Public domain.
130	The Metropolitan Museum of Art/Public domain.
133	The Jewish Museum/Public domain.
134	The Jewish Museum/Public domain.
136	Web Gallery of Art/Wikimedia commons/Public domain.
143	ivan-96/DigitalVision Vectors/Getty Images.

Other Graphic and Texture:
FlamingPumpkin/Getty Images.
Lubushka/iStock/Getty Images.
Vectordivider/iStock/Getty Images.

NOTES